Jacobs
The rise a
struggles o
American civ
rights

E DUE

The RISE and STRUGGLES of

AMERICAN CIVIL RIGHTS

AUTHORS and CONSULTANTS

DONALD M. JACOBS, Ph.D.
Assistant Professor of History
Northeastern University
Boston, Massachusetts

ARVARH E. STRICKLAND, Ph.D.
Professor of History
University of Missouri

F. C. BARTONE, Ph.D.
Supervisor, University Division
of Instructional Services
Pennsylvania State University
University Park, Pennsylvania

ILLUSTRATORS and GRAPHIC ARTS

Simon Mezerow • Curt Parkhouse • Walter Whirl • Arnie Kohn
Warren Tufts • Richard Potts • Sol Dember • Harry Blumenthal
Joseph Postilion • James Axelrod • Gail Goldberg • William Gray
Steven Dobson • Andrew Stefani

UNITED STATES HISTORY SOCIETY, Inc.

CHICAGO, ILLINOIS U.S.A.

Introduction

"We hold these truths to be self-evident, that all men are created equal; that they are endowed by their Creator with certain unalienable rights..."

The Declaration of Independence

it has been almost 200 years since Thomas Jefferson wrote these inspiring words for the Declaration of Independence. When they were composed they were approved and applauded by his co-signers of the Declaration and by men of good will everywhere. But few Americans in those years realized the full significance of the words *"all men"* included in this important document. No one can say with certainty what our fathers had in mind when they included the words *"all men"*, but historians today are able to look back at the feelings and backgrounds of the many colonists involved in the writing of the Declaration, and from this conclude that *"men"* meant to them those people who had similiar European backgrounds. The Indian red man and the African black man were not seriously considered.

AMERICA'S FIGHT FOR UNALIENABLE RIGHTS

An age old struggle of man has been to hold an equal share, or to have an equal opportunity to obtain his share, in the rights and benefits offered by his country.

In attempting to cover the *Rise and Struggles of American Civil Rights*, the authors and consultants realized from the beginning that their most difficult task was in the manner of selection. The objective of this book is to be able to evaluate the thousands of events that took place in nearly two hundred years of America's struggle for equality, and to place each event in its meaningful, historical perspective. The editors have tried not to overemphasize any distinct minority viewpoint, regardless of its purpose. Instead, it was their hope to present the history of a whole people.

The multi-racial and multi-ethnic society that makes up the fiber of America is the principal reason for America's advancement in the fields of technology, economy, education, and social justice. It is the differences of the American people—color, religion, background—that have influenced our thinking, our actions and our laws. Looking back at the civil and social customs, political legislation, and court decisions that were practiced in America, men and women everywhere will agree that some should not have been tolerated. But so many of the events that took place reflected the attitudes of many of the people at that time.

It is the hope of educators that each succeeding generation will be better informed, more sensitive to the plight of their fellow human beings and more encouraged to seek solutions, than were their fathers and forefathers.

Hopefully, the development of freedom as presented in this volume will reach young people everywhere, and provide them with an overview of the background of the struggle for American rights. Possibly no subject today is as relevant to America's future citizens as is civil rights.

The New World Attracted People from the Old World

America was discovered and many unhappy and oppressed people moved from their old countries to a new one. They journeyed to America with the hopes of a newer and freer life. Others, including the Spaniards, came to find riches.

England established the Thirteen Original Colonies which became the start of the United States of today. Some English settlers came to find new homes. Others came to escape religious persecution, and others to avoid going to prison for debts. The Englishmen brought with them strong belief in the rules of the Magna Charta (Great Charter) which King John signed in 1215. It guaranteed some personal liberties for the English people.

The French came to hunt , fish, trap and build up a fur-trading empire. Some people of other nationalities also came to the New World: Italians, Swedes, Irish, Jews, Germans, Dutch, and Asians. For most of them, the New World held a promise of happier homes, with more rights and freedoms awaiting their arrival.

One group that did not always come to America of its own free will was the Negro. In the beginning, Negroes accompanied and gave assistance to the explorers Columbus and Balboa and the Spanish conquerors Cortez and Pizarro. But the great mass of Negroes came as captives, purchased in their native Africa and taken to America in slavery chains.

SELF-RULE by white settlers and bringing in of captive black men both began in America in the same year and at the same place. In 1607, Jamestown was founded by the London Company under a land grant, or permission, given by King James I of Britain. The company and its governors ruled the colony with a strong hand. The colonists protested loudly. Finally, in 1619, the London Company gave in and allowed the government in America to change many laws. Jamestown was put under the rule of two law making groups. One was a council of state made up of the governor and other London Company representatives. The second group was the House of Burgesses, made up of free citizens called burgesses, who were chosen by the people.

Self-rule by white settlers —first arrival of black men

Jamestown was divided into eleven communities, called "cities" or "hundreds." Each group chose two representatives. On July 30, 1619, the House of Burgesses held its first meeting, with twenty-two representatives attending. The meeting, held in a church, lasted several days. Laws were passed by the burgesses ordering punishment for idleness, Sabbath-breaking, drunkenness and gambling. It was the first meeting of representatives of the English colonies ever held in North America. The beginning of self-rule which the Virginians won became a pattern that other colonies would follow.

In that same year—1619—the first Negro workers were taken to Jamestown. A Dutch ship landed twenty African captives in the colony. The Dutch had taken the Negroes from a Spanish slave ship. They offered the human cargo for sale so cheaply that the Jamestown planters bought the Negroes. The growing of tobacco was big business in Jamestown and the Negroes were needed as workers on the tobacco farms. Some of the African captives were put to work in the fields and others were put to work in Jamestown homes.

The Negroes were not all slaves in the seventeenth century. They were listed in early court records as indentured servants, or people bound-out to work. After working for a certain number of years as unpaid and unfree servants, some of the Negroes were given their freedom. But over a period of many years, as more Africans were brought to America and economic changes took place, slavery slowly began to take a firm hold.

Pilgrims set own rules in Mayflower Compact

A HOPE for religious freedom brought the second group of colonists to America. In 1620, the Pilgrims arrived in the New World and settled at Plymouth in what now is Massachusetts. Plymouth was the second and final stop on the Pilgrims' journey from England to the New World. They had left the Church of England over different religious beliefs and were known as Separatists. England's King James I said of those who opposed the Church: "I will make them conform (accept the rules), or I will harry (punish) them out of the land." In 1609, about 100 of the Separatists moved to Holland, on the first stop of their trip to religious freedom. After ten years, they wanted a home of their own and, in 1619, obtained a grant of American land from the Virginia Company (formerly London Company). The Pilgrims stopped off at Plymouth, England, and picked up additional members before sailing to America. A total of 102—73 men and 29 women and children—crossed the Atlantic Ocean in the *Mayflower* and arrived off the coast of Massachusetts in November, 1620.

Before landing, forty-one of the Pilgrims signed a historic agreement known as the Mayflower Compact. It bound the Pilgrims together in a "civil body politic." It provided for the passage of such just and equal laws as were thought best for the good of the colony. Adoption of the Mayflower Compact was the first time American colonists set their own policies and laws without having an English governor.

Another group of unhappy English church members landed in America in 1628. They were the Puritans and they settled at Salem, Massachusetts. In 1630, other Puritans founded Boston. John Winthrop was elected governor of the new Massachusetts Bay Colonies. The Puritans did not want to break completely with the Church of England. On arrival in America, they set up a strict religious system of their own, including rules for personal conduct. Those who broke the rules were punished. The punishments included ducking women in ponds, locking men in wooden hand and foot blocks, and lashing the more serious offenders at public whipping posts. Many personal freedoms were denied the people, including being too loud and too merry in public.

THE PURITANS themselves "harried" or punished those who did not agree with their beliefs. A young pastor named Roger Williams was one target of their religious punishments. After arguments about religion, Williams left Boston and went to Plymouth, but there he had other arguments with the Pilgrims. Finally, in 1635, the Massachusetts General Court (assembly) ordered Williams sent out of Massachusetts. He fled to the forests, and was taken in and helped by Indians. In the spring of 1636, Williams set out with a few followers determined to build a colony where each man could worship according to his own wishes and beliefs. Williams and his party bought land from the Indians at the head of Narragansett Bay. There they founded Providence. Other villages were built by Williams and followers of Anne Hutchinson, another religious "rebel" who had been driven from Massachusetts. As Williams had preached, the government of his new colony was separated from the church. The colonists were not forced to attend church. They could engage in any trade and there were no restrictions on the right to vote. Although Williams opposed Negro slavery, slave trading did develop in southern Rhode Island.

Other beginnings of freedom were planted in a Maryland Colony. Lord Baltimore obtained a "proprietary," or almost personal type of charter to land in the Chesapeake Bay area. In 1634, Baltimore's son sent "twenty gentlemen and 200" laborers to the area, which was named Maryland in honor of England's Queen Mary. They built a town on the shores of Chesapeake Bay and named it St. Mary's. The Baltimore proprietor at first attempted to have only the upper class, or only those people with property and money, rule. But that soon changed. Lord Baltimore's charter stated that Maryland's government should be "subject to the advice

and consent (agreement) of the people.".

Lord Baltimore's family were Catholics, and Maryland was to be a safe home for persecuted English Catholics. But more Protestants than Catholics turned up as the original settlers and soon more Protestants joined them. Though the Toleration Act of 1649 gave limited religious freedom, problems soon developed between the Catholics and Protestants. At no time were people other than Christians allowed in the colony.

Democracy in America had its start in Pennsylvania

THE QUAKERS were another strongly persecuted group in England. Other Englishmen talked against the Quakers because they insisted on peace and "would not fight." William Penn, a young Quaker church member, founded a colony for Quakers in present Pennsylvania. Penn obtained a large land grant from King Charles II in payment of a family debt of 16,000 pounds (English money). The land was in the Delaware River region and King Charles named it Pennsylvania, or "Penn's Woods." In 1681, Penn sent an advance group which founded the city of Philadelphia,which means Brotherly Love. Penn arrived the following year with 100 settlers, and began establishing one of America's first truly democratic governments, or government by the people.

Complete religious freedom was granted to all. Penn signed a "Great Treaty" calling for peace with the Indians. He announced a "Frame of Government" which ignored hard colonial laws ordered by the king. Penn established provincial, or regional, rule by a one-house legislature elected by the people. A list of rules called the "Great Law" was adopted, guaranteeing that there could be no unfair government. All land owners were given the right to vote. Prisoners who broke the laws were ordered to reform, work and learn trades. The laws prohibited disorderly conduct, duelling, drunkenness and lying. Only disloyalty to the government and murder were punishable by death.

Pennsylvania settlers were the first group of white American settlers to protest against Negro slavery. In 1688, the Mennonites, a religious order of Germantown, Pennsylvania, issued a protest, stating: "What thing in the world can be done worse to us, than if men would rob or steal us away, and sell us as slaves to strange countries?" They said that Negro slaves had a right to fight for freedom.

American colonists' anger against rule by British governors already was beginning to rise. In 1676, Governor William Berkeley of Virginia refused to send troops to put down an Indian uprising on the frontier. Nathaniel Bacon, a young burgessman (assemblyman), organized a force and defeated the Indians. Berkeley declared that Bacon was leading a revolt. On their return from the Indian battle, Bacon and his men found the governor's troops waiting.

Bacon defeated the governor's troops and burned Jamestown. Bacon died later from an attack of fever and Bacon's Rebellion died with him. But the uprising helped correct some wrongs and dishonesty in Virginia's government, and King Charles II of England recalled Berkeley.

Democracy Took Root in American Soil

The right to make laws and establish public offices was stated by the Pilgrims in adopting their Mayflower Compact. The Compact, signed while aboard ship, marked the beginning of self-determination, or self-government, in the colonies.

Self-rule had become established as the goal of the settlers. The colonists had brought with them a strong desire to rule themselves and enjoy personal liberty.

Religious liberty was begun when Roger Williams founded Rhode Island in 1636. Men worshipped as they wished.

Only twelve years after founding of the colony, Jamestown elected its own assembly. The House of Burgesses was established as the first move toward government representing the town citizens.

The first formal constitution in the American colonies was adopted by Connecticut as the Fundamental (basic) Orders. Many personal freedoms were granted.

Resistance to British Rule Gained Strength—

As the Eighteenth Century advanced, England passed laws and taxes which the colonists disliked. A desire for freedom grew.

The American criticism of British rule gained a powerful new weapon—freedom of the press (1734). John Peter Zenger, New York printer and editor, was jailed after criticizing New York Governor William Cosby. Zenger was freed when his lawyer, Andrew Hamilton, shouted to the jury: "This is not the cause (fight) of just one poor printer, it is the cause of liberty." The courtroom crowd cheered.

British tax agents used Writs of Assistance to search and seize property suspected of being smuggled goods. These writs were general search warrants, or legal papers, which could be used anywhere at any time. Many colonists were arrested on charges of smuggling, or slipping in goods without paying taxes. They were defended (1761) by James Otis, whose arguments for liberty included opposition to slavery. The colonists lost the case, but Otis' reasoning advanced the cause of independence.

After the French and Indian War, England raised taxes in the colonies. In 1765, a Stamp Act was passed, requiring tax stamps on legal papers, newspapers, and many licenses. A colonist resistance group was formed, called the Sons of Liberty. Mob violence broke out. The Sons of Liberty destroyed government property and threatened hangings. The colonists refused to buy British goods, and England's merchants lost much trade. The act was ended by England in 1776.

On March 5, 1770, the Boston Massacre took place. A crowd of Boston townsmen gathered at a British customs house. A sentry was shoved about. Snowballs were thrown at the soldiers. A gun was discharged; the British fired on the rioters and five colonists were killed—the first Americans to die in the Revolution. A leader of the crowd and one of those killed was Crispus Attucks, a runaway Negro slave who had become a seaman.

—America's Revolution for Freedom Was Won

Resentment brought revolution. Revolution brought independence. The great fight of the colonists brought about the United States of America.

England passed new restrictions which the colonies called the Intolerable (unbearable) Acts. One act most bitterly hated was the closing of Boston's port (June 1, 1774) after the Boston Tea Party.

Washington and the American army suffered many defeats in the first years of the war. But in 1777 they were able to defeat the British armies moving down from Canada. The end came on October 19, 1781, when British General Cornwallis surrendered to George Washington at Yorktown. The peace treaty signed on September 3, 1783, declared the "Thirteen United States" free and independent.

Patriots met at Philadelphia and on July 4, 1776, approved the Declaration of Independence declaring the colonies free from England. "We hold these truths to be self-evident", the signers said, "that all men are created equal; that they are endowed by their Creator with certain unalienable rights...Life, Liberty and the pursuit of happiness." The big break!

The thirteen United States ratified, or approved, a new government under the Constitution on June 21, 1788. A strong central government was established, under a President, a Congress and a court system. On April 30, 1789, George Washington commander of the American army, took the oath as the first President.

The Bill of Rights Guaranteed Personal Freedoms

THE BILL OF RIGHTS was ratified on December 15, 1791, and was to guarantee the individual freedoms of all Americans. They were added to the Constitution as the first ten amendments. Five states had ratified the Constitution only upon being promised that the Bill of Rights would be added. Many basic rights of the citizens were included, and there were guarantees of protection against legal and governmental injustices. These guarantees included in the Bill of Rights have never been changed.

THIRD. No soldier, in time of peace, shall be given living room in any house without the house owner's consent.

FIRST. Freedom of religion, speech and the press are guaranteed. People have the right to appeal to the government.

FOURTH. The people cannot be subjected to search of homes or seizure of property without specific legal warrants.

SECOND. A well-regulated militia being necessary, people have the right to keep arms. (Strong laws prohibit abuses).

FIFTH. No person can be tried for a major crime without an indictment. He can also refuse to testify against himself.

SIXTH. In all criminal prosecutions, the accused has the right of a speedy public trial occuring before a fair jury.

SEVENTH. In suits at common law, where the value in dispute exceeds $20, a person has the right of a jury trial.

EIGHTH. Excessive bail, fines and cruel or unusual punishment are not allowed.

NINTH. The listing in the Constitution of certain rights cannot be taken to mean that other rights are denied the people.

TENTH. Powers not given to the federal government by the Constitution, and not ruled out by it, belong to the states.

The Constitution and Bill of Rights failed to cover fully the civil and human rights that belonged to the people. For Americans, no exact standards were set for voting privileges and women's rights. For the black Americans, these and other rights were ignored. The pressing and cruel injustice of slavery remained.

The first governmental step against the slave trade was begun, however. The Constitution allowed Congress to act against foreign slave trade after 1808. During Thomas Jefferson's last year as President, Congress passed a law to stop the shipping of slaves to the United States on and after January 1, 1808.

DURING AND AFTER the Revolutionary War, the slaves' rights to freedom began to be recognized— particularly in the North. During the war, many free Negroes and slaves served in the colonial armies. After the war, large numbers of these slaves were rewarded with their freedom. Anti-slavery societies were formed to speed the movement to free the slaves and their families. John Jay, patriot statesman, in 1785 headed a New York Society for Promoting the Manumission (freeing) of Slaves. While the Revolutionary War was still in progress—in 1780—Pennsylvania passed a law providing for the gradual ending of slavery in the state. No Negro born after that date could be held in bondage for more than twenty-eight years as an indentured servant.

Anti-slavery laws, or steps taken to end slavery, were passed early in some northern states. By 1783, Massachusetts courts had ruled against slavery. Connecticut and Rhode Island passed acts in 1784 providing for slavery to be ended over a period of years. New York had an effective anti-slavery law in force by 1799 and New Jersey had one by 1804. While public feeling against slavery was rising in the North, Southerners still held to the belief that slaves were necessary for their section's prosperity. Much money was invested by the South in the slaves and their services on cotton and tobacco plantations and farms were considered necessary.

The fight to keep slavery out of the territories of expanding America also had begun. In 1787, Congress passed the Northwest Ordinance. One provision stated that neither slavery nor involuntary servitude would be permitted in the Northwest Territory. In Northern states, the number of free Negroes, as compared to slaves, had risen to a marked degree by 1790. Of 50,000 Negroes living in the Middle Atlantic States, 14,000 were free. In the New England states, only 1,700 of the 13,000 Negroes living there were slaves. Massachusetts and Vermont had no slaves at all.

America Was Headed on a Long Journey Toward Equal Rights

Full personal rights and equality were still distant goals, but a start toward them had been made by the end of the Nineteenth Century's first quarter. The Bill of Rights gave many Americans guarantees of personal liberties, but some of their rights were still unprotected.

Religious freedom, which began in Rhode Island and Pennsylvania, had spread throughout the colonies. The state and church were separated, leaving religion to the individual's own personal choice.

Voting rights remained a limited privilege controlled by state laws. Some states still had laws permitting only property owners to vote. The winning of full voting rights for all adult Americans, regardless of race, color or sex was to become a very long and sometimes bitter fight.

Freedom of the press was recognized even before the Bill of Rights. As early as 1734, John Peter Zenger, New York editor-printer, had won a case against the British governor, opening the way for the writing of fair criticism of leaders.

Anti-slavery sentiment already had swept through the North. Groups campaigning for the ending of slavery were formed and protest meetings were held. In the South, with the growth of cotton farming after Eli Whitney's invention of the cotton gin, slavery became more widely established as more Negro field workers were used to plant and grow the cotton.

David Walker's appeal for freedom of slaves

SOME NEGROES living in the United States gained freedom before the Civil War. Many ran away or were given their freedom by their masters. Some became educated and held good positions and some campaigned earnestly and strongly for freedom for all Negroes in America. One such freedman was David Walker, who was the agent in Boston for the first Negro newspaper in America, the New York *Freedom's Journal.* In 1829, Walker addressed an *Appeal* to the people of the United States. It was an appeal, or plea, for freedom for the black people. Walker told Negro slaves they had the right to rise in bloody rebellion if they were not given freedom. Walker closed his *Appeal* with:

"Remember, Americans, that we must and shall be free and enlightened (educated) as you are, will you wait until we shall, under God, obtain our liberty by the crushing arm of power? Will it not be dreadful for you? I speak, Americans, for your good. We must and shall be free, I say, in spite of you. You may do your best to keep us in wretchedness (poverty) and misery, to enrich you and your children, but God will deliver us from under you. And woe, woe will be to you if we have to obtain our freedom by fighting. Throw away your fears and prejudices (unfairness) then, and enlighten and treat us like men, and we will like you more than we do now hate you, and tell us no more about colonization (in Africa), for America is as much our country as it is yours.

"Treat us like men, and there is no danger but we will all live in peace and happiness together. For we are not like you, hardhearted, unmerciful, and unforgiving. What a happy country this will be, if the whites will listen...But, Americans, I declare to you, while you keep us and our children in bondage (slavery), and treat us like brutes, to make us support you and your families, we cannot be your friends. And yet there is not a doubt in my mind, but the whole of the past will be sunk into oblivion (forgetfulness) and we yet, under God, will become a united and happy people. The whites may say it is impossible, but remember that nothing is impossible with God." Walker's *Appeal* attracted wide attention.

OPPOSITION to slavery grew into an organized abolition movement in the North—and into violence on some slave-holding plantations in the South. In August, 1831, Nat Turner, a Negro preacher, organized and led a slave uprising in Southampton County, Virginia. David Walker had written in his *Appeal* that slaves were justified in rising in bloody revolt if they were not granted freedom. Turner's uprising was bloody. Fifty seven white men, women and children were slain. An estimated 100 Negroes were killed as punishment for the rebellion. Many had not even been involved.

Turner's uprising was well organized. The slaves of several plantations fell in with his plans, and runaway slaves hiding out in swamps were reported to have joined them. The rebellion struck on a Sunday night, when many of the white men were attending a meeting in another county. Entire families were attacked and slain by the slaves. The next morning, the white planters made an appeal to Fort Monroe for federal troops. State militia were called. A total of about 300 troops joined in a manhunt for the rebel slaves. Nearly all of the rebels were tracked down in the woods and swamps. But Nat Turner was not captured then. After two months, he was captured while hiding in a small cave which he had dug out under a fallen tree. The captured slave rebels were tried and twenty were sentenced to death. Among those put to death was Turner.

The slave rebellion frightened Virginians and proposals were made to give up slavery. A convention was held during the winter of 1831-1832 and several proposals for emancipation were voted down. Instead, the convention took steps to tighten the rules to prevent another slave revolt. The slaves' movements were controlled and they were not permitted to attend meetings. In the North, an organization to help slaves escape from the South developed. This organization was called the Underground Railroad. It was not a real railroad, but a network of secret roads, paths and hideouts. Negroes often participated in helping others escape.

Indian tribes were moved from their lands to territories

RED MEN at this same time were being denied rights along with the black men. Whereas the Negroes had been forced to come to America, the Indians were forced to give up lands which for hundreds of years they had called their own. On becoming President in 1828, Andrew Jackson adopted a policy of removing the defeated Indian tribes to territories, or special lands set aside for them. The tribes fought against being moved from their hunting grounds and home fields. More than fifty years of bloody wars were to follow. The first purpose of the territorial policy was to clear out the Indians in the East and Southeast and move them to territories in Oklahoma. During Jackson's administration (1829-1837) the government put pressure on the Indians and ninety-four treaties were signed with Indian tribes.

Unlike other groups, the Indians were not recognized as citizens of the United States. Indian tribes were treated as separate nations. Treaties were made with them as with any other separate country. They ruled and governed their own nations except in matters connected with their territorial lands.

Among the first tribes to give in and agree to move were the Choctaws and Chickasaws in Mississippi, and the Cherokees and Creeks in Georgia and Alabama (1830-1838). The Seminoles of Florida held out the longest. Jackson had fought the Seminoles and the Creeks and was fully aware of their ability to fight back.

Hard treatment by the states and the lack of federal help finally beat down the Indians of the East. The red man had few rights in white man's courts. Some white men's laws allowed lawsuits to collect Indian debts, but some would not let Indians come to trial and defend themselves in court. The U. S. government signed a treaty recognizing the Cherokee Indians as a separate nation. But soon settlers from Georgia, Alabama and Mississippi began moving into the Indian territories. The Cherokees sued the State of Georgia in the U.S. Supreme Court to make the state stop its moving in on the Indian lands. The Court refused to stop the State of Georgia from taking over the land. The Court decision said the Cherokees were a "domestic, dependent nation" and not considered as a foreign country. Therefore the federal court had no power to rule on the case.

Indian warfare moved westward as white men pushed farther out from the East. Later, the Wars of the Great Plains brought bloody fights with such tribes as the Sioux, Comanches, Apaches, Arapahoes. Cheyennes, Kiowas and Navajos. The wars brought defeats to more tribes, and the removal of more Indians to special reservations, or lands laid out by the government just for the Indians.

William Lloyd Garrison led fight to free slaves

WILLIAM LLOYD Garrison stepped forward as leader of the Abolitionist anti-slavery movement when he published the first issue of *The Liberator* (one who sets free) in Boston on January 1, 1831. Week after week, *The Liberator* published articles by Garrison. In Boston, Garrison became the target of the anti-abolitionists. He was shouted down at public meetings. On October 21, 1835, a Boston mob seized Garrison and dragged him through the streets of the city. He was almost killed, but continued his attacks on slavery.

Garrison had been a young newspaperman in his hometown of Newburyport, Massachusetts. He became co-editor of the *National Philanthropist*, a reform paper, in Boston. Garrison then moved to Baltimore as co-editor of *The Genius of Universal Emancipation*. In 1830, he was sent to prison as a result of his articles. Garrison's fine was paid by Arthur Tappan, a New York abolitionist sympathizer. With Isaac Knapp, he founded *The Liberator* in Boston and announced his policy: "I will not retreat a single inch. And I will be heard!" Garrison organized the American Anti-Slavery Society.

Anti-slavery societies sprang up throughout the North and Middle West. Oberlin College, in Ohio, the first American college to admit women, decided to admit Negro students. Theodore Weld, an anti-slavery leader, helped spread the movement in the Middle West. He encouraged students at Lane Theological Seminary at Cincinnati to join the crusade. Many of the students went to Oberlin, which became a key "station" of the Underground Railroad. The Underground Railroad used large wagons as "trains." Several runaways could hide in each wagon. The wagons traveled over back roads. Homes where the runaways were fed and helped along were called "stations." Both whites and Negroes served faithfully to help the slaves escape from bondage and find new homes—and freedom—either in the North or in Canada. Levi Coffin, Indiana banker and Quaker, hid runaway slaves in his own home.

Congress was so swamped with anti-slavery protests that it voted a "gag rule," accepting no more protests. Former President John Quincy Adams, then in the House of Representatives, said the "gag rule" deprived the people of their constitutional right of protesting to the government. But Congress still would not consider the thousands of petitions against slavery.

23

THE REVEREND Elijah P. Lovejoy, a white newspaper editor, knew what terrors the abolitionist movement faced. Anti-abolitionist feeling often turned into violence. Meetings of anti-slavery societies were broken up. Lovejoy had been driven out of Missouri and the printing press of his abolitionist newspaper had been thrown into the river. Moving to Alton, Illinois, Lovejoy addressed a public meeting and announced that he intended to print an anti-slavery newspaper.

On November 7, 1837, anti-abolitionist rioters attacked Lovejoy's printing plant. They began destroying the press. Lovejoy tried to defend his press and was killed. Several members of the mob were charged with the murder, but all were freed. The Reverend Lovejoy was regarded as a martyr, or one who gave up his life to defend a cause, for freedom of the press. The story of Lovejoy's killing brought thousands of new members to the abolitionist movement.

THE WOMEN'S rights movement in America had its active beginning when the first convention was held at Seneca Falls, New York, in 1848. The leaders were two outspoken fighters for women's rights and against slavery. They were Elizabeth Cady Stanton and Lucretia Coffin Mott. Many rights enjoyed by men were denied women at the time. They did not have the right to vote. There were limits on their education and their ownership of property. Women were stopped from entering such professions as medicine and law. Into this fight for women's rights stepped Mrs. Stanton and Mrs. Mott, both mothers of large families and both good housekeepers.

Elizabeth Cady was a New York reformer who had married Henry Brewster Stanton, an anti-slavery leader. Lucretia Coffin was a Quaker who was a minister in the Society of Friends. She married James Mott, a teacher. In the beginning, abolition of slavery had been the major goal of Mrs. Stanton and Mrs. Mott. In 1840, a world anti-slavery convention was held in London. Henry Stanton attended the convention accompanied by his wife. In London, Mrs. Stanton met Lucretia Mott and several other women leaders from America. The convention refused to recognize them as delegates, or official members, because they were women. Then and there was born the idea of a women's rights movement in America. Mrs. Mott and Mrs. Stanton agreed to call a national convention upon their return home.

The convention at Seneca Falls, New York, took place on July 19-20, 1848, in the Wesleyan Methodist Church. Mrs. Stanton startled other leaders when she announced she was introducing a resolution demanding voting rights for women—almost unheard of at that time. Mrs. Stanton found a backer among the delegates—Fredrick Douglass, an important Negro leader in the Nineteenth Century. Douglass made a strong speech in support of the resolution. It was adopted along with ten other resolutions, and women's long, hard journey on the road to equal rights was under way.

Sojourner Truth told the men about women's rights

THE WOMEN'S rights crusade struggled on in the years leading up to the Civil War. Another convention was held in May, 1851. Elizabeth Cady Stanton, Lucretia Mott and other leaders attended. Also present were Negro supporters. In the course of the convention, a tall, powerful black woman rose from her seat and made her way to the platform. She was Sojourner Truth. In a low, deep voice she made a speech which held the listeners spellbound. She made her point perfectly clear—if women wanted to "turn the world rightside up" by insisting on their rights, the "men had better let them do it!" Sojourner Truth, a former New York slave who helped give hope to her race, returned to her seat amid applause.

Mrs. Stanton met Susan Brownell Anthony, a social reformer, in 1851 and caused her to join in the women's rights crusade. For many years, they worked together but made slow progress. They conducted campaigns and made many speeches, often together. After the Civil War, Susan B. Anthony joined in the campaign for Negro voting rights. In 1869, she became president of the National Woman Suffrage Association. Women were first heard by a state lawmaking body on February 8, 1860. Mrs. Stanton gave an address before the New York state legislature. Her subject was women's right to vote. Mrs. Stanton told the legislators of the injustice of denying women the vote.

Women had made some gains in other fields by then. Dr. Elizabeth Blackwell was accepted by the medical profession. Margaret Fuller, literary editor of the *New York Tribune*, was outspoken for women's rights. Another leading woman reformer was Dorothea L. Dix of Boston. She campaigned to ease the conditions of insane persons who were kept in prisons. Mrs. Dix investigated the conditions under which the insane were kept in Massachusetts jails. She spread her crusade across the country and in three years visited 18 state prisons, 300 county jails and more than 500 almshouses, or poor houses. Her efforts began a movement to have the mentally ill prisoners sent to hospitals or asylums. The campaign led to state-supported hospitals for the insane in 15 states and in Canada. People soon began to look into other prison conditions.

Harriet Tubman was "Moses" to the black people

AMERICA'S QUARREL over slavery rose to violent levels in the ten years leading up to the Civil War. Bitter fighting marked the struggle in the "Bleeding Kansas" Territory. White abolitionists gained in strength throughout the North. An increasing number of escaped slaves were helped to freedom over the Underground Railroad. A Negro woman rose to fame among her people—Harriet Tubman. An escaped slave, she was called the most daring Underground Railroad "conductor" in the 1850's. Mrs. Tubman was given credit by some with making 19 trips into the South after her own escape and leading 300 slaves back North to freedom. Thomas Higginson, a minister and abolitionist, wrote in 1859: "We have the greatest heroine (brave woman) of the age here, Harriet Tubman, a black woman and a fugitive (runaway slave). She has been back eight times (up to then) secretly and brought out in all 60 slaves with her, including all her own family, besides aiding many others to escape. Her tales of adventure are beyond anything in fiction and her ingenuity (smartness) and generalship are extraordinary (very unusual) . . . the slaves call her Moses. She has had a reward of $12,000 offered for her in Maryland and probably will be burned alive whenever she is caught." Harriet Tubman was never caught. She served the Union in the Civil War as a spy and nurse. Late in life, in 1898, she began receiving a pension of $25 a month. The pension payments began thirty years after Harriet Tubman first requested them. She based her claim on Union Service.

Harriet (Moses) Tubman once explained her feelings: "I grew up like a neglected weed—ignorant of liberty, having no experience of it. I was not happy or contented; every time I saw a white man I was afraid of being carried away. I had two sisters carried away in a chain gang—one of whom left two children. We were always uneasy. Now I've been free. I know what slavery is. I have seen hundreds of escaped slaves but I never saw one who was willing to go back and be a slave . . . I think slavery is the next thing to hell. If a person would send another into bondage, he would, it appears to me, be bad enough to send him to hell if he could."

Dred Scott decision caused new controversy THE DRED SCOTT case brought the courts into the slavery fight. Scott was a Negro slave who had been taken to live in free territory. He sued for his freedom, but the U. S. Supreme Court denied Scott's plea. The decision, given in 1857, angered the anti-slavery North and pleased the South's slave holders. Dred Scott, the Negro slave, was owned by Doctor John Emerson of Missouri. Scott was taken by his owner first to Illinois and then to Wisconsin Territory. Illinois was a free state and slavery was prohibited, or ruled out, in Wisconsin Territory by the Missouri Compromise of 1820. Scott remained on free soil most of 1834-1838. After Doctor Emerson's death and after being taken back to Missouri, Scott sued for his freedom on the grounds that he had lived on free soil and therefore was considered a free man. A lower court in Missouri decided in Scott's favor, but the state's supreme court reversed the ruling.

The Scott case finally reached the U.S. Supreme Court with John F. A. Sanford, Scott's new owner, as defendant. The Supreme Court had to decide whether Scott was a citizen of the State of Missouri, which would give federal courts the power to rule on his constitutional rights. The court also had to decide whether Scott's stay on free soil had made him free. The constitutionality of the Missouri Compromise also would be questioned. Scott lost his case when the Supreme Court ruled against all three points.

Each Supreme Court justice gave a separate opinion, but the one generally accepted as speaking for the majority was written by Chief Justice Roger B. Taney of Maryland. Taney said that Scott was not a citizen of Missouri or of the United States, because he was a Negro slave and not considered a citizen of Missouri under that state's slave laws.

The court said freed Negro descendants of slaves could be citizens of states recognizing them as free, but that the Constitution denied them any national citizenship. This meant they had no rights in federal courts and were strictly under the power of the state courts where they lived. The ruling was meant to cover all Negro slaves and their descendants. Scott was declared not free because the state in which he filed suit (the slave state Missouri) governed his status, or standing. The Missouri Compromise was unconstitutional, the court ruled, because it violated, or was against, the Fifth Amendment, which guaranteed the property rights of U. S. citizens. The court also ruled that Scott, the slave, was his owner's property, and the Missouri Compromise could not take property away from its owner. The Supreme Court dismissed Scott's suit on the grounds that, because he was not a citizen protected by the Constitution, the United States federal courts could not interfere with the decision made by the Supreme Court of Missouri.

Abraham Lincoln's Emancipation Proclamation

LINCOLN'S Emancipation Proclamation, made on January 1, 1863, during the Civil War, declared all slaves held in areas still in rebellion to be free. There had been much demand in the North to "free the slaves." On August 19, 1862, Horace Greeley, editor of the *New York Tribune*, published a letter as an editorial. Titled *Prayer of Twenty Millions*, the editorial urged the President to "free slaves in rebel areas." On September 17, an invasion attempt by Robert E. Lee's Southern army was turned back in the Battle of Antietam. Lincoln had been waiting for a Union victory to give him a timely opportunity to make a declaration of freeing the slaves. On September 22, Lincoln announced in a Preliminary Proclamation that he would issue his Emancipation Proclamation on January 1, 1863. It was announced on schedule.

Lincoln declared that all slaves held in rebellion areas were "then, thenceforward (from then on) and forever free." Few slaves actually were freed at the time. Lincoln's order could be enforced only in regions captured and held by Union troops. But Lincoln had taken the step that would lead to the freeing of all slaves. The Proclamation also served an important military purpose—some anti-slavery European nations had been thinking about entering the war on the side of the South. Lincoln's Emancipation Proclamation made them sympathetic to the ideals of the North. The European nations gave up all ideas of opposing the Union.

Lincoln made his proclamation as commander-in-chief of the United States armed forces. In this form, the act was a "fit and necessary (needed) war measure." It halted possible constitutional and congressional troubles. Congress already had done away with slavery in the U. S. territories by an act of June 19, 1862.

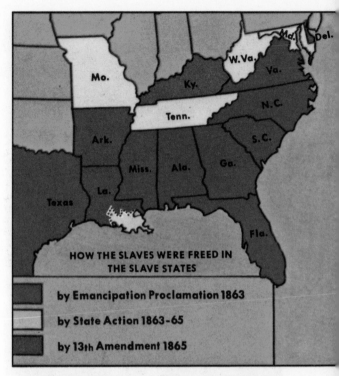

HOW THE SLAVES WERE FREED IN THE SLAVE STATES

by Emancipation Proclamation 1863

by State Action 1863–65

by 13th Amendment 1865

In the South, large numbers of Negroes remained at their old homes with their masters' families. Many slaves, however, escaped to the North and others accompanied returning Union raiding parties. After the Emancipation Proclamation, Negroes were invited to join the Union ranks as soldiers and many responded. About 180,000 Negroes volunteered by the end of the war. This made up between nine and ten per cent of total Union enlistments. The Negroes fought in 499 military engagements. Thirty-nine of the engagements were major battles. The death toll among the Negro soldiers was high, a total of 68,178 killed in action. This was more than one-third of the total who had volunteered to fight for the Union.

29

Thirteenth
Amendment
ended slavery
in America

life became a bitter struggle. New homes, food, clothing and other family needs had to be arranged for. Congress had begun to prepare for this when it had created a Freedmen's Bureau in March, 1865. The Bureau gave quick help to the freed Negroes, as well as to many whites. In four years, 15 million rations of food were issued to Negroes and 5 million to whites. The Bureau established 46 hospitals and more than $2,000,000 was spent on the health care of the freedmen. Educational aid was given at day and night schools, with large numbers of teachers from the North taking over classes. Great progress was made on Negro education during the Reconstruction period.

The Freedmen's Bureau distributed some land to the freedmen in small parcels and some land was used as areas for the sick and penniless. But the great problem was that no base was set up for the Negro to be able to support himself in the future. Temporary relief helped with the immediate problems, but plans for the freedman's long range ability to support himself through his own free labors were not made. Without land to work and with little opportunity to acquire a job, many freed slaves had to return to the farms—little or no better off than they were before the war.

Some leaders in Congress pressed demands for more punishment of the South. Charles Sumner, Republican senator from Massachusetts, said that the Southern states had committed "state suicide" and should be treated as territories. Thaddeus Stevens, congressman from Pennsylvania, called the South "conquered (defeated) provinces." Stevens was a leading opponent of slavery. He once paid $300 out of his own pocket to buy freedom for a slave who was about to be sold away from his family. As a lawyer, he defended many fugitive slaves without charge. Stevens proposed giving each freed Negro a parcel of land from the "conquered territories."

ALL SLAVES were legally freed by the Thirteenth Amendment. The amendment was adopted by Congress on January 31, 1865, before the Civil War ended. It became effective on December 18, after approval by twenty-seven states. The Thirteenth Admendment stated "Neither slavery nor involuntary servitude, except as punishment for crime whereof the party shall have been duly convicted, shall exist within the United States, or any place subject to their jurisdiction (rule)." Slavery had been ended in America, but its memories, hatreds, hardships and the results of its injustices long were to remain.

With the ratification, or approval, of the Thirteenth Amendment, life did not turn immediately into the dream of happiness for which so many slaves had hoped. For many

Some States Forced Black Codes on the Freed Slaves

By the end of 1865, after ten per cent of their voters took oaths of loyalty to the union, all former Confederate states except Texas had formed their own governments. Black Codes then began to make their appearance. The codes were laws passed by the new state governments which denied Negroes civil rights guaranteed by the Freedmen's Bureau. The Black Codes placed Negroes in a lower legal and social class. The first Black Code was passed by the state of Mississippi in November, 1865.

If he could not pay the $50 vagrancy fine, the Negro could be "apprenticed," or bound out, to a farmer for six months. Often, the particular farmer had been the slave's former owner. Northern congressmen complained that the former slave was still bound to work on the land.

The state governments which adopted Black Codes claimed that their purpose was to aid and protect the Negroes. The former slaves were not used to earning a living and taking care of themselves, Many of the Southern legislators said.

Most of the Black Codes provided for Negroes to be fined $50 if found guilty of vagrancy, or not working. Some codes called a former slave guilty of "vagrancy" if he were not working for a white man.

Northern Congressmen called the codes a scheme by the South to get around the Thirteenth Amendment's order ending slavery. Foes of the Black Codes called them the next thing to the former slavery.

Civil Rights Act of 1866 was the nation's first

THE FIRST Civil Rights Act, known as such and aimed directly at Negroes' rights, was passed by Congress in 1866. The act was first passed on March 13, less than three months after the Thirteenth Amendment giving slaves their freedom was approved. President Andrew Johnson vetoed, or turned down, the Civil Rights Act on March 27. Congress promptly overrode the veto on April 9 to make the

law official and final. At the same time, another bill was passed by Congress over an earlier Johnson veto. This bill kept the Freedmen's Bureau alive.

The major purpose of the Civil Rights Act of 1866 was to give citizenship to Negroes born in the United States. In 1857 the Supreme Court had ruled that Dred Scott was not a citizen of the United States because he was a Negro slave. The 1866 act provided for Negroes to have the same rights as whites and to have equal benefits of the laws. Another part gave the President the power to use federal armed forces, land or naval, to enforce the act.

In his veto, President Johnson said that the act was against states' rights. Also, he said that the right to use armed forces "establishes for the security (safety) of the colored race safeguards (defenses) which go infinitely (far) beyond any that the General Government has ever provided for the white race." Doubts soon arose about the Civil Rights Act of 1866 being constitutional. Republican radicals in Congress also wanted to put the provisions of the act beyond the power of a later Congress to make changes. A movement began to try and include some of the same laws into a Constitutional Amendment— the Fourteenth. As matters turned out, the 1866 act remained effective and, 102 years later, the Supreme Court used the act to support Negroes' open housing demands.

Court ruled military trials of civilians illegal

THE RIGHT of military authorities to put civilians on trial in areas far away from actual war zones was denied by the U. S. Supreme Court in an 1866 decision. The case was *ex-parte Milligan*. It involved an Indiana civilian named Milligan, who was arrested by Union troops in 1863 at Indianapolis, Indiana. He was tried by a military commission, convicted of trying to stir up a rebellion, and was sentenced to be hanged. The Supreme Court's decision, written by Justice David Davis of Illinois, attacked military trials of civilians in areas where the civil courts were open and available to hear such cases. The court ruled that the Constitution guarantees trial by civil jury of any accused person who is not attached to the military services. Milligan was set free by the Supreme Court decision.

Justice Davis, reviewing the case, said: "Milligan, not a resident of one of the rebellious (Confederate) states, or a prisoner of war, but a citizen of Indiana for twenty years past, and never in the military service, is, while at his home, arrested by the military power of the United States, imprisoned, and, on certain criminal charges preferred (made) against him, tried, convicted, and sentenced to be hanged by a military commission, organized under the direction of the military commander of the military district of Indiana. Had this tribunal (commission) the legal power and authority to try and punish this man?...

"Every trial involves the exercise (use) of judicial (court) power; and from what source did the military commission that tried him derive (obtain) their authority? Certainly no part of the judicial power of the country was conferred on them; because the Constitution expressly (directly) vests (puts) it in 'one Supreme Court and such inferior (lower) courts as the Congress may from time to time ordain (plan) and establish.' " Justice Davis pointed out that Indiana was not threatened by a Confederate invasion and was not under martial or military law. He said that Milligan should have been turned over to the civilian court of Indiana for trial.

2 amendments gave Negroes citizenship, voting rights THE FOURTEENTH and Fifteenth Amendments were ratified, or approved, by the states, guaranteeing Negroes civil and voting rights. The Fourteenth Amendment, passed by Congress in 1866 and ratified in 1868, repeated many of the laws listed in the Civil Rights Act of 1866. All Negroes born in the United States were included as citizens and had the same rights as all other citizens and equal protection of the laws. No citizen could be denied these rights without due process of law, or proper legal steps. The long, uphill fight for Negroes' equal civil rights had its real beginning with the Fourteenth Amendment.

The amendment prohibited the holding of public office, civil or military, by any former Confederate who before the war had taken an oath of office under the Union. The public debt, or money owed by the United States, was declared to be legal, but the war debts of the Confederacy and all of its states were not to be paid by the government. Claims for payment for the loss of slaves were declared illegal. Ratification, or approval, of the amendment was required before a Confederate state would be taken back into the United States. Tennessee ratified the amendment but the other Southern States refused. Union troops were soon moved into the South to register Negro voters as Congress now took control of Reconstruction. New state constitutions were written and passed and new governments were elected which ratified the Fourteenth Amendment.

Adult Negro men qualified for voting rights with the ratification of the Fifteenth Amendment in March, 1870. The amendment said: "The rights of citizens of the United States could not be denied or abridged (cut down) by the United States or by any individual state on account of race, color or any previous condition of servitude (slavery)." This included Negroes. After the other states ratified the Fifteenth Amendment, Mississippi, Virginia, Texas and Georgia were forced to ratify before they would be readmitted to the Union. Georgia also was forced to readmit Negroes kept out of its state legislature. With Georgia's readmission in July, 1870, all eleven of the former seceded states were back in the Union. But Union troops still stayed in the South and controlled Reconstruction. Seven more years were to pass before the last Union troops were to be recalled from the South.

Congress heard a direct plea for women's voting rights ELIZABETH Cady Stanton, as a leader in the women's suffrage fight, finally made a direct plea to Congress for women's voting rights. As Ulysses S. Grant began his first term as President in 1869, the Fifteenth Amendment, assuring voting rights for Negro men, was still up before the states for ratification, or approval. Mrs. Stanton and her co-campaigners were trying to have laws passed that women's voting rights also could not be denied. Who could and could not vote was decided by the states. The states could give women the right to vote if they wanted to. But women wanted a federal law giving women the vote. Congress granted Mrs. Stanton a committee hearing. On January 23, 1869, Mrs.

Stanton and Susan B. Anthony appeared before a committee in the Senate. They were politely received and listened to, but fifty more years were to pass before Congress finally gave voting rights to women.

Some progress was being made however. In December of that same year, Wyoming Territory passed a women's voting law, the first state or territory to do so. Mrs. Stanton campaigned strongly for more women's rights. She was co-editor of the *Revolution*, a weekly women's rights newspaper. Starting in 1869, Mrs. Stanton also spent eight months a year traveling and making speeches throughout the country. Though woman's rights was a favorite subject, so were a woman's duties as housewife and mother. Mrs. Stanton also talked on training children. She raised seven.

Act of 1875
gave Negroes
equal public
services
NEGROES FOR A time had legal rights to equal services with whites in public places, as a result of the Civil Rights Act of 1875. The act, passed by Congress on March 1, ordered that, regardless of color, all persons should be given equal rights and services in such places as inns, restaurants and theaters, and on trains and buses, or coaches. The act also prohibited, or ruled out, the keeping of Negroes from jury duty. The Civil Rights Act of 1875 stood up for eight years, until ruled unconstitutional in 1883.

The Civil Rights Act had stated: "Whereas it is essential to just government, we recognize the equality of all men before the law, and hold that it is the duty of government in its dealings with the people to mete out (provide) equal and exact justice to all. . .Be it enacted, that all persons within the jurisdiction (rule) of the United States shall be entitled to full and equal enjoyment of the accomodations (things needed), advantages, facilities, and privileges in inns, public conveyances (transportation) on land or water, theaters, and other places of public amusement; subject only to the conditions and limitations (limits) established by law, and applicable (applying) alike to citizens of every race and color, regardless of any previous condition of servitude."

The Civil Rights Act of 1875 also provided "that no citizen possessing all other qualifications which are or may be prescribed (outlined) by law shall be disqualified (ruled out) for service as grand or petit (lower) juror in any court of the United States, or of any state, on account of race, color, or previous condition of servitude." Legally, Negroes were given these equal rights, but when many Negroes tried to make use of the new privileges, they were still denied the services in many places.

Court killed 1875 act as "based on social rights."

THE DENIAL OF equal services resulted in the filing of lawsuits by Negroes. Five cases, appealed from lower courts, reached the Supreme Court. In each case a Negro had been denied the services and privileges ordered by Congress in the Civil Rights Act of 1875. In its decision, the Supreme Court ruled the Civil Rights Act of 1875 unconstitutional. The major reason given was that the law attempted to give Negroes social rather than civil rights and that the federal government had no power to control or rule on social rights.

The Supreme Court ruled that the denial of services to Negroes at inns, restaurants and theaters did not violate the Fourteenth Amendment because that amendment was written to deal with state laws and not with the social actions of individuals. And, as the Negroes who were appealing were not being forced back into slavery, the Supreme Court ruled there was no violation of the Thirteenth Amendment. The court's decision said, "We are forced to the conclusion (decision) that such an act of refusal has nothing to do with slavery or involuntary servitude... It would be running the slavery argument into the ground to make it apply to every act of discrimination (keeping out) which a person may see fit to make as to the guests he will entertain or as to the people he will take into his coach or cab or car, or admit to his theater..."

Supreme Court Justice John Harlan of Kentucky strongly disagreed with the decision. He argued that the rights covered by the act were not social rights but civil rights. Negroes are citizens, of the state, that licenses these inns, restaurants and theaters, he pointed out. They are used by the public and "...license from the public imports (gives) equality of rights at such places among all members of the public."

Harlan asked, "What was secured (given) to colored citizens by the national grant of state citizenship? There is one right if there be no other: exemption from race discrimination in respect of any civil right belonging to citizens of the white race in that same state. I agree that government has nothing to do with social, as distinguished from legal, rights of an individual. The rights which Congress by the Act of 1875 endeavored (wanted) to protect are legal, not social rights. The right of a colored person to use the accommodations (inns) of a public highway upon the same terms as are permitted to white citizens is no more a social right than his right, under the law, to use the public streets of a city or town or a turnpike or postoffice... The Civil Rights Act of 1875 is for the benefit of citizens of every race and color. Today, it is the colored race which is denied, by corporations and individuals holding public authority, rights fundamental to their freedom and citizenship. There cannot be in this Republic, any class, with power to dole (give) out to another just such privileges as they may choose to grant."

The Supreme Court's decision ended almost all federal government efforts to enforce the Fourteenth Amendment until the Twentieth Century.

Ku Klux Klan and "Jim Crow" laws brought new violence THE TROUBLED decade of the 1870's and 1800's brought new setbacks in the black man's struggle for equality and justice. During President Grant's administration, some Southern whites rose against Reconstruction—the post-Civil War rebuilding of the South. They formed secret societies to terrorize "carpetbaggers," Northerners who went into the South. The most feared terrorists were the Ku Klux Klan, organized soon after the war by ex-Confederate soldiers at Pulaski, Tennessee. Former Confederate General Nathan B. Forrest was the first Grand Wizard, or top leader. The Ku Klux Klan spread across the South. The Klansmen wore white robes and masks. They whipped, covered with tar and feathers, and even killed some persons picked out for "punishment." They attacked Negro militia. Many "carpetbaggers" fled back North. Negro leaders often went into hiding. Congress passed two Ku Klux Klan acts to put down the terrorists and enforce the Fourteenth and Fifteenth Amendments. Grant used the power of his office to bring hundreds of Klansmen to trial, but the Klan could not be broken.

Rutherford B. Hayes became President in 1877 after an election which both he and Samuel J. Tilden claimed to have won. Hayes, a Republican, was chosen President by a special electoral commission which decided the matter. Hayes promised the Democrats that he would withdraw federal troops from the South, ending Reconstruction. As President he ordered the last federal troops to leave the South. They were withdrawn by April, 1877. Before the troops were withdrawn, white Democrats were already in control of most southern state governments.

Soon troubles began for Negroes and new racial problems were stirred up. "Jim Crow" laws were passed in the South. The first was passed in 1881 by Tennessee. The "Jim Crow" laws denied Negroes equal rights in riding on public means of travel. The first law said that Negroes had to ride in separate sections on trains. Later, as other states passed "Jim Crow" laws, buses and streetcars were included. Negroes were placed in separate sections, usually in the back of the bus, and Negroes could not use a seat unless the seat was not needed for a white man or woman. Florida, Mississippi, Texas and Louisiana soon followed Tennessee's lead by passing "Jim Crow" laws. It was the beginning of legal segregation—in time to become one of America's bitterest issues.

Indians offered chance to own their own farms PROBLEMS AND situations of the American Indians were discussed by President Chester A. Arthur in his First Annual Message in 1881. Many bloody Indian wars had been fought in the West following the Civil War. Most tribes had been defeated and thousands of Indians sent to special reservations where the Indians had become an abandoned people. Moved by their problems, the President said: "I refer...to the government's policy of dealing with the various Indian tribes as separate nationalities, of relegating (removing) them by treaty stipulation (terms) to the occupancy of immense (huge) reservations in the West, and of encouraging them to live a savage life, undisturbed by any earnest and well directed efforts to bring them under the influences of civilization...We have to deal with the appalling (alarming) fact that thousands of lives have been sacrificed and hundreds of millions of dollars expended (spent) in the attempt to solve the Indian problem, and it has until the past few years seemed scarcely nearer a solution than it was half a century ago."

President Arthur urged Congress to take steps to improve the Indian situation. He called attention to efforts which had been made to pass a law giving individual Indians, if they chose, the right to leave their tribes and obtain farm lands of their own. Arthur asked Congress to pass such an act, and said: "There is reason to believe that the Indians in large numbers would be persuaded to sever (cut away) their tribal relations and engage at once in agricultural (farm) pursuits." In 1887, Congress passed the Dawes Severalty (separation) Act, which was a move to break up these Indian tribes.

The Severalty Act provided for lands on reservations to be divided into individual farms and offered to individual male Indians living on the reservations. Each head of an Indian family was offered 160 acres. Each single Indian over 18 was offered 80 acres. Each orphan child under 18 was to be given 80 acres, and all other single Indians under 18 were to receive 40 acres. The Indians who received the farm lands under the Severalty Act could not sell or get rid of the lands for 25 years. The lands would be held in trust by the U. S. government for the use and benefit of the Indians living on them. Those Indians who renounced, or gave up, their tribal connections and obtained Severalty Act lands were granted United States citizenship.

Frederick Douglass: his goals and career

THE FIGHT to improve the lives of the Negro people and the protest against their poor treatment were pushed by Frederick Douglass. He had been a former Negro slave and a leader in the fight for emancipation. In the 1880's, about 75 per cent of the Negroes in the United States lived in the South. With living conditions in the South offering them little chance for improvement, many Negroes began moving to the North. This was the beginning of what was to develop into the Great Migration, or movement. Frederick Douglass was against large scale movement. He said the government should protect citizens everywhere—North or South. Douglass did not believe Negroes would gain in the long run by moving. He feared they might become wanderers.

Douglass devoted his entire career to advancement of the Negro people and service to his country. He was born in Maryland in 1817, the son of a white father and a Negro slave. As a youth, he escaped from a farm to the North. Douglass established an abolitionist newspaper, *The North Star*. He was forced to flee to Canada when he was accused of plotting with John Brown, leader of the Harper's Ferry Revolt in 1859. Douglass was a loyal supporter of the North in the Civil War and Reconstruction period. He assisted President Lincoln in forming two Massachusetts Negro regiments during the war. He served in the District of Columbia legislature during Reconstruction years.

Douglass held many government posts, including secretary of the Santo Domingo Commission. He reached a high point in his governmental career in 1889 when President Benjamin Harrison appointed him as Minister Resident and Consul General to the Republic of Haiti. Douglass later was named Charge d'Affaires for Santo Domingo. Throughout his lifetime Douglass had also supported women's rights.

During Reconstruction, the first Negroes were admitted to Congress in 1870. Joseph H. Rainey of South Carolina won a seat in the House and Hiram R. Revels of Mississippi became the first Negro senator. In his first Senate speech, Revels said: "Members of my race aim not to elevate (raise) themselves by sacrificing one single interest of their white fellow citizens."

Negroes were soon accepted in other fields. In 1875, James Augustine Healy became the first Negro Catholic bishop in the United States, heading a diocese, or district, including Maine and New Hampshire. His brother, Patrick Francis Healy, was president of Georgetown University.

Supreme Court decision set "separate but equal" policy

A "SEPARATE but equal" doctrine, or policy, in providing places of public service for Negroes was established by the U.S. Supreme Court in 1896. The doctrine was contained in a decision in the court case of *Plessy versus Ferguson*. It upheld a Louisiana "Jim Crow" law requiring separate railroad coaches for white and black riders. The majority opinion, or decision by the larger number of judges, was written by Justice Henry B. Brown of Michigan. It said that the law requiring separate places did not "destroy the legal equality of the two races, or reestablish a state of involuntary servitude." Such laws, the decision said, "do not necessarily imply (suggest) the inferiority (lower class) of either race to the other."

Separate schools for white and black children were given as examples. The Supreme Court ruling said that such separated schools "have been held to be a valid (lawful) exercise (use) of the legislative power even by courts of states where the political rights of the colored race have been longest and most earnestly enforced." The decision concluded: "If the civil and political rights of both races be equal, one cannot be inferior to the other civilly (as citizens) or politically."

Justice John M. Harlan of Kentucky wrote a dissenting, or disagreeing, opinion. He said that the law in question was against "the personal liberty enjoyed by every one within the United States." His dissenting report said: "The destinies (fates) of the two races in this country are indissolubly (strongly) linked together, and the interests of both require that the common (same) government of all shall not permit the seeds of race hatred to be planted under the sanction (approval) of law. What can more certainly arouse race hate, what more certainly create and perpetuate (carry on) a feeling of distrust between these races, than state enactments (laws) which in fact proceed on the ground that colored citizens are so inferior and degraded (lowered) that they cannot be allowed to sit in public coaches occupied by white citizens?"

The "separate but equal" doctrine as handed down by the Supreme Court was to remain in force for more than fifty years.

41

Booker T. Washington's Atlanta Compromise

THE NEGROES' social conditions and lack of basic skills for advancement were pointed out by Booker T. Washington, important Negro educator. Washington had moderate civil rights policies in keeping with his times. In 1895, he made a speech, known as the Atlanta Compromise (agreement for peace), which troubled some Negro leaders. Addressing a Cotton States fair, Washington said:

"A ship lost at sea for many days suddenly sighted a friendly vessel. From the mast of the unfortunate vessel was seen a signal: 'Water, water, we die of thirst!' The answer from the friendly vessel at once came back: 'Cast down (drop) your bucket where you are'. . . (after delays, the bucket finally was cast down) and it came up full of fresh, sparkling water. . . To those of my race who depend on bettering their condition in a foreign land, or who underestimate the importance of cultivating (developing) friendly relations with the Southern white man, who is their next door neighbor, I would say: 'Cast down your bucket where you are'—cast it down making friends in every manly way of the people of all races by whom we are surrounded.

"Cast it down in agriculture, mechanics, in commerce (business), in domestic service, and in the professions. . . Our greatest danger is that in the great leap from slavery to freedom we may overlook the fact that the masses of us are to live by the production of our hands, and fail to keep in mind that we shall prosper (make gains) in proportion (the same rate) as we learn to dignify and glorify common labour and put brains and skill into the common occupations (work) of life. . . No race can prosper till it learns that there is as much dignity in tilling (plowing) a field as in writing a poem. It is at the bottom of life we must begin, and not at the top. Nor should we permit our grievances (complaints against wrongs) to overshadow our opportunities (chances).

"To those of the white race. . . were I permitted I would repeat what I say to my own race: 'Cast down your bucket where you are.' Cast it down among the 8,000,000 Negroes whose habits you know, whose fidelity (loyalty) and love you have tested. . . Cast down your bucket among these people who have, without strikes and labour wars, tilled your fields, cleared your forests, builded your railroads and cities. . . In all things that are purely social we can be as separate as the fingers, yet one as the hand in all things essential (needed) to mutual (both) progress.

"There is no defense or security (safety) for any of us except in the highest intelligence (wisdom) and development of all. . . Nearly sixteen million hands will aid you in pulling the load upward, or they will pull against you the load downward. We shall constitute (make up) one-third and more of the ignorance and crime of the South, or one-third its intelligence and progress. . . The wisest among my race understand that the agitation (stirring up) of questions of social equality is the extremest folly (greatest foolishness). . . It is important and right that all privileges of the law be ours, but it is vastly more important that we be prepared for the exercises (use) of these privileges. The opportunity to earn a dollar in a factory just now is worth infinitely (far) more than the opportunity to spend a dollar in an opera house."

W. E. B. DuBois was a leader in the Niagara Movement

WILLIAM E. B. DUBOIS, Negro scholar and author, took a forceful view of his people's struggle for civil rights. In 1903, DuBois in his book, *The Souls of Black Folks*, wrote: "In the history of nearly all other races and peoples the doctrine preached...has been that manly self-respect is worth more than lands and houses, and that a people who voluntarily surrender (willingly give up) such respect, or cease striving (trying) for it, are not worth civilizing.

"**In answer to this,** it has been claimed that the Negro can survive (continue to live) only through submission (giving up). Mr. Washington (Booker T.) distinctly asks that black people give up, at least for the present, three things—political power, insistence on (demands for) civil rights, higher education of Negro youth—and concentrate (center) their energies on industrial education, the accumulation (piling up) of wealth, and the conciliation (friendship) of the South...As a result of this tender (offer) of the palm-branch, what has been the return? (Since Washington's Atlanta speech) there have occurred: disenfranchisement (taking away the vote) of the Negro, the legal creation of a distinct status (standing) of civil inferiority (lower class), the steady withdrawal of aid from institutions for the higher training of the Negro. These movements are not, to be sure, direct results of Mr. Washington's teachings, but his propaganda (ideas) has, without a shadow of a doubt, helped their speedier accomplishment...

"**Negroes do not expect** that the free right to vote, to enjoy civic rights, and to be educated, will come in a moment; they do not expect to see the bias and prejudices (unfair policies and attitudes) of years disappear at the blast of a trumpet; but they are absolutely certain that the way for a people to gain their reasonable rights is not by voluntarily throwing them away and insisting that they do not want them; that the way for a people to gain respect is not by continually belittling and ridiculing (making fun of) themselves; that on the contrary (just the opposite) Negroes must insist continually, in season and out of season, that voting is necessary to proper manhood, that color discrimination is barbarism (uncivilized), and that black boys need education as well as white boys...

"**By every civilized** and peaceful method we must strive (work) for the rights which the world accords to men...life, liberty and the pursuit of happiness."

Dubois was a graduate of Fisk University and received a doctor of philosophy degree from Harvard. In 1905, DuBois, then a professor at Atlanta University, headed the first Negro protest organization formed in the Twentieth Century. He and other Negro leaders met at Niagara Falls, New York and began the Niagara Movement. The Negroes met on the Canadian side, where hotels were open to them. The Niagara Movement was against the Atlanta Compromise policy of Booker T. Washington. DuBois and his fellow leaders adopted a policy of pressing for the immediate winning of civil rights for all Americans. DuBois said: "We are men! We will be treated as men. And we shall win!"

Negro leaders helped influence U.S. Presidents NEGROES' HOPES for obtaining a stronger recognition of their civil and citizenship rights rose as the Nineteenth Century turned into the Twentieth. By the year 1900, William McKinley had named many Negroes to U. S. government positions. Only a month after becoming President upon McKinley's assassination in 1901, Theodore Roosevelt invited Booker T. Washington to dine with him at the White House and discuss the nation's racial problems. Southern newspapers and congressmen attacked the "social meeting between whites and blacks," while some Northern newspapers replied that the South was angry because Roosevelt's action might lead to an end of the South's "wicked reign of terror" against Negroes.

Booker T. Washington's relations with Presidents Roosevelt, William Howard Taft and Woodrow Wilson continued on a friendly and helpful basis. He also was active politically and gave advice on Negro matters. In 1903, Roosevelt appointed William D. Crum, a leading Negro citizen, to the collector's position at the Port of Charleston, South Carolina. The *Coloured American Magazine* called Crum's appointment the Negroes' "greatest political triumph in twenty years." President Taft ap-

pointed William H. Lewis of Boston, a Negro, as Assistant U. S. Attorney General. President Wilson named Robert H. Terrell of Washington, also a Negro, judge of the District of Columbia municipal court.

The Negroes' hopes of great gains under the Roosevelt-Taft-Wilson administrations fell short of being fulfilled, however. During a wave of race riots early in the 1900's, Roosevelt shook the Negroes' confidence by his handling of a riot at Brownsville, Texas, in 1906. Three companies of the Negro Twenty-fifth Regiment exchanged shots with whites, and one white was killed. An inspector's report blamed the Negroes for the riot and President Roosevelt dismissed all members of the three Negro companies without honor and without the right to reenlist. An uproar in Congress followed and, three years later, a court of inquiry was ordered. The court ruled that all of the discharged Negro soldiers who qualified for reenlistment could now reenlist, with back pay to the date of their discharge.

In Woodrow Wilson's first year as President, many bills proposing laws that discriminated against Negroes were introduced in Congress. Few of the bills passed, but Wilson set back civil rights by an executive order that established segregated eating and rest-room facilities for most of the Negro federal employees.

A national association was formed to advance Negroes

THE NATIONAL Association For the Advancement of Colored People was formed in 1909—growing out of the Niagara Movement. The Association (N.A.A.C.P.) was organized in New York on February 12, Abraham Lincoln's birthday. Many well known names in the civil rights fight were listed among the supporters. In addition to William E.B. DuBois, Negro leaders included Archibald H. Grimke, Alexander Walters, Ida Wells Barnett, Mary McLeod Bethune and Mary Church Terrell. White supporters included John Dewey, Jane Addams, Lincoln Steffens, William Dean Howells, Mary White Ovington, Ray Stannard Baker, Lillian Wald, Rabbi Stephen Wise and William English Walling.

The N.A.A.C.P. grew rapidly and by 1914 had established fifty branches throughout America. The *Crisis,* a magazine edited by DuBois, became the official publication for the N.A.A.C.P. From its beginning, the association was a powerful fighter for Negro rights and equality. Building up strong local and legal organizations, the N.A.A.C.P. gained many of its goals largely through legislation, educational campaigns and civil law suits. It became a strong and important spokesman for the black citizen.

A Great Migration, or movement, of Negroes from the farming South to big cities in the North began in 1915. World War I had begun in Europe, and America's plants and factories were working night and day to fill European orders for war supplies. A big demand arose for new workers and Negroes hurried to leave the farms and get jobs in the factories. In a few years, some one million Southern Negroes joined the Great Migration from their Dixie farms.

Negroes turned to parading as a means of gaining the public's support in their fight against wrongs. In 1917, some 10,000 Negroes marched down Fifth Avenue in New York to protest the lynchings, or killings, of Negroes by mobs in the South. DuBois and James Weldon Johnson, poet and diplomat, were among the leaders of the march. The National Association for the Advancement of Colored People conducted a long campaign for a federal law against lynchings. In 1919, the association published *Thirty Years of Lynching in the United States, 1889-1918.* The number of lynchings during the period that the book exposed shocked Americans everywhere. In 1921, the N.A.A.C.P. sponsored more than 200 protest meetings in various cities. But little resulted, as no federal laws were passed against lynching.

Jeannette Rankin—the first woman in Congress

A MAJOR GAIN in women's fight for equal rights was made by Jeannette Rankin of Montana. In 1917, she was elected to the House of Representatives as the first woman member of Congress. Miss Rankin's career began on a Montana ranch and carried her to many places as a leader in the fight for women's voting rights. Miss Rankin served as a congresswoman from 1917 to 1919. She did not run for reelection to the House. Instead, she chose to seek the Republican seat in the Senate. Although defeated, she had only begun her career of helping women add their influence to the running of the government.

Jeannette Rankin was born on June 11, 1880, on a ranch near Missoula, Montana. From 1908 to 1909, she attended a New York School for training social workers.

Jeanette Rankin turned to the women's voting rights crusade. From 1910 to 1914, she campaigned in Montana, Washington and California. She was elected field secretary of the National American Woman Suffrage Association and was chairman of the Montana State Suffrage Committee. Miss Rankin was a persuasive speaker and was the main speaker at many suffrage meetings. To gain knowledge of social conditions in other parts of the world, she made a trip to New Zealand in 1915.

The first woman to win her way to Congress, Jeannette Rankin blazed the trail for many women to follow.

Amendment finally gave women full voting rights

WOMEN FINALLY won full rights to vote! On August 26, 1920, the Nineteenth Amendment was ratified by the states, adding women's voting rights to the Constitution. The amendment stated: "The right of the citizens of the United States to vote shall not be denied or abridged (cut down) by the United States or any state on account of sex." The long fight finally had been won. Seventy-two years had passed since Lucretia Mott and Elizabeth Cady Stanton had conducted the first Women's Rights Convention in 1848. Wyoming, while still a territory, had been the first state to legalize women's suffrage—in 1869. By 1919, fifteen states had passed similar laws. Montana legalized the women's vote in 1914 and, three years later, elected Jeannette Rankin as the first woman member of Congress.

Equality of the sexes, or equal rights for men and women, was now established in political as well as business and social fields. Women, who long had provided a large number of factory workers, now were employed in many office "white collar" jobs. During World War I, a call went out for women and girls to fill necessary jobs in war plants. Thousands answered the call and the sight of women hurrying to work, with their dinner pails under their arms, became a familiar one on the American scene.

After winning full voting rights, women lost little time in making their influence felt in that area. It was estimated that only twenty-six per cent of the eligible women voted in the 1920 election, but the percentage steadily increased in following Presidential elections. The estimate for the 1968 election was sixty per cent. Women introduced many new steps in the political process. Included were nonpartisan (favoring neither party) registration and "get out the vote" campaigns—to assure more representative elections.

Ku Klux Klan rose again in a reign of terror

GHOSTS OF the past—the Ku Klux Klan—rose again to terrorize both whites and blacks in 1915. The dreaded secret order, presumed dead since Reconstruction days, was said to have been revived, or put back in action, at a meeting on Stone Mountain near Atlanta, Georgia, in November, 1915. The Twentieth Century Klan stirred up prejudices, or unfair beliefs, and urged white, Protestant rule over all others. It chose its targets from among the Negroes, Catholics, Jews and foreigners and terrorized them. The victims faced torture and sometimes murder. In the early 1920's, the Klan claimed to have 5,000,000 members with control over several state governments in the South.

The public was shocked in 1923 when Eastern newspapers published stories on the Klan. The *Baltimore Sun* made public Klan terrors in Morehouse Parish, Louisiana. It was charged that a grand jury had refused to bring some white persons to trial, even when accused of murder. A New York newspaper printed charges against Edward Clarke and Mrs. Elizabeth Taylor, leaders of the Klan. The newspaper's reports spotlighted the Klan's activities and brought demands for jailing Klan members. The Klan's large membership dropped rapidly. But the Ku Klux Klan still was not yet destroyed. . . it was due to rise again as a force that would fight civil rights gains.

N.A.A.C.P. Won 3 Early Cases in the Supreme Court

After its organization in 1909, the National Association for the Advancement of Colored People carried its fight for Negroes' rights to the courts. Three important cases were won in the U.S. Supreme Court in the N.A.A.C.P.'s early years of seeking rights.

Some states had "grandfather clauses" in their constitutions. This clause had given voting rights to adult men whose grandfathers or fathers had been qualified to vote on January 1, 1867. This was an additional block to Negro voting rights. In the 1915 case of *Guinn versus United States*, the Supreme Court ruled that "grandfather clause" in the Oklahoma constitution violated the Fifteenth Amendment, and, therefore, the law was illegal.

In 1917, the Supreme Court said a Louisville, Kentucky, law which forced Negroes to live in certain sections of the city set apart for them was illegal. This case was *Buchanan versus Warley*.

In 1923, a new trial was ordered for a Negro convicted of murder in Arkansas. In the *Moore versus Dempsey* case, the Supreme Court ruled that the Negro had not received a fair trial because Negroes were not permitted to serve on the jury.

Another advance during this period was the organization in 1911 of the National League on Urban Conditions among Negroes, better known as the National Urban League. This league was formed as a merger of three other Negro groups. The Urban League sought new opportunities for Negroes in industry and helped them with their urban, or city, problems after moving from farm areas to cities.

WORLD WAR I brought a new struggle for Negroes —a fight for full civil rights as they fought for their country. By the end of the war, hundreds of thousands of Negroes were in service, 1,400 Negro officers had been commissioned and assigned to duty, and many Negroes had won medals for bravery in battle overseas. But World War I Negro soldiers also fought hard to overcome military discrimination. At the outbreak of war, there were 20,000 Negroes among 750,000 men in the Regular Army and National Guard. There were four Negro units in the regular army—the Ninth and Tenth Cavalries and the Twenty-fourth and Twenty-fifth Infantries. There were no Negroes in the Marines and only a scattering of Negroes in the enlisted ranks of the navy.

When America declared war on Germany in April, 1917, large numbers of Negroes rushed to volunteer, but generally they were not accepted. Some 700,000 Negroes reported on the first day of registration for the draft, July 5, 1917. In all, 2,290,525 Negroes registered for the draft, and about 367,000 of them were called into service, many with combat units. Negro soldiers made up the Ninety-second and Ninety-third combat divisions. Negroes were always kept within all-Negro units. Their of-

ficers were both whites and Negroes. Four infantry regiments of the Ninety-third were assigned to fight with the French. The Negro 369th was the first Allied regiment to reach the Rhine River in Germany.

Strong arguments and the support of 300 Congressmen were needed to persuade the army to establish a separate training camp for Negro officers. Many camps had already been established for white officers. The camp was finally established at Fort Des Moines, Iowa, and in October, 1917, 639 Negroes were commissioned as captains, first lieutenants and second lieutenants.

Many racial problems accompanied the Negroes as they went into the service. To help solve them, Secretary of War Newton D. Baker appointed as his special assistant Emmett J. Scott, who had been Booker T. Washington's secretary for eighteen years. Discrimination by white troops and officers and by local townspeople brought some serious incidents. In South Carolina and Texas racial incidents turned into riots and sometimes shootings. Facilities for recreation also caused problems for Negro troops in the South. Scott went out to investigate charges of unfair treatment. He also advised on the draft, and helped Negroes in matters of war risk insurance and army allowances and pay. Scott's war time services, both to Negroes and the army, were praised.

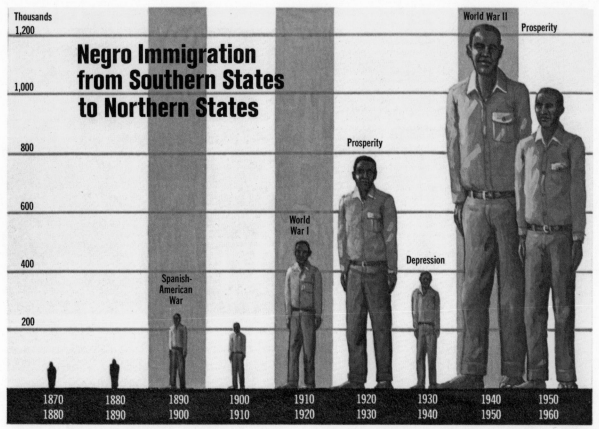

Negro Immigration from Southern States to Northern States

Thousands										
1,200										
1,000										
800										
600										
400										
200										

Spanish-American War

World War I

Prosperity

Depression

World War II

Prosperity

1870 1880	1880 1890	1890 1900	1900 1910	1910 1920	1920 1930	1930 1940	1940 1950	1950 1960

Negroes hurried to help fill wartime job needs

THE GREAT Migration of Negroes from the South to the North reached higher levels during World War I. A severe pre-war depression in the South and poor cotton crops increased the Negroes' desires to seek better opportunities. With the outbreak of World War I, northern industry went into massive production. The demands for wartime materials grew each month. The need for more workers increased with greater production demands. Immigration to the U.S. had fallen off sharply after 1914. During the World War I period, many hundreds of thousands of Negroes migrated from the South.

The Department of Labor established a Division of Negro Economics to help meet the wartime problems. George Edmund Haynes was the director. The division advised the Labor Department and federal bureaus on policies which would help the Negro perform wartime duty under im-

proved conditions. The division also sought good relations between Negro and white workers and their employers. Most Negro workers were anxious to work hard on their new jobs. They were involved in many types of work. They helped produce guns, ammunition and the iron and steel products needed to win the war. More than 25,000 Negroes worked in shipyards turning out warships and merchant vessels. Many thousands of Negro women also worked in the war plants.

The National Urban League formed in 1911, aided the Negroes' efforts in the Great Migration and war resettlement. New housing had to be obtained. Recreation programs had to be arranged for the Negro workers and their families. The Urban League opened offices in such cities as Detroit, Chicago, St. Louis, Cleveland, Philadelphia and Pittsburgh. The league also helped steer the Negro newcomers to centers where they would find the best job opportunities.

51

Race rioting, violence followed World War I RACE RIOTING which had built up during World War I broke out in full violence in 1919. The Ku Klux Klan had been revived in the South and West. The Klan had a strong hand in the lynching of seventy Negroes, including a dozen soldiers still in uniform, during the first year after the war. During the last six months of 1919, twenty-five race riots took place in American cities. In July, Longview, Texas, was the scene of a large-scale riot. Many white men entered a Negro section of the town hunting for a Negro school teacher who was suspected of sending a newspaper story to Chicago about the lynching of a Negro. Several white men were shot and other whites charged into the Negro community seeking revenge. Some homes were burned and several Negro leaders were chased out of town. Rioting continued for several days.

Washington, the nation's captial, became another major riot scene a week later. Newspaper stories accusing Negroes of mistreating white women aroused Washington whites. Sailors, soldiers and Marines led white mobs in three days of rioting in the streets. Several Negroes were killed and dozens of others injured. The Negroes rose in force on the third day when a mob tried to burn homes and wreck property in the Negro section of Washington. Casualties were high on both sides before this battle ended, after which the rioting stopped.

Late in July, 1919, the costliest riot of all took place at Chicago. The disorder began when a Negro swimmer in Lake Michigan ventured into water off a beach which was reserved for whites. Some whites threw rocks at the young Negro and he sank and drowned. When the victim's body was recovered it showed no signs of having been struck by stones. But the riot already had begun and was spreading through the city, as the result of wild rumors of heavy fighting on the beach. White and Negro mobs gathered in several parts of the city and there was fighting throughout the night. Although the state militia was called out on the fourth day, Chicago was torn by violence for thirteen days. By the time the rioting ended, 38 persons had been killed—15 whites and 23 Negroes. A total of 537 were injured—178 whites, 342 Negroes, and 17 whose racial identity was not listed. Nearly 1,000 Negroes were homeless after house burnings and wreckage of property.

Negroes faced union problems in job hunting

NEGROES' employment opportunities declined during the ten years following World War I. There were more Negro workers but fewer jobs were available. With the ending of war production, the plants cut down their working forces. Many Negroes turned to other fields, such as the automotive industry, transportation and communications. But the Negroes faced the problem of union membership. The United Mine Workers was one of the few unions which welcomed Negro members without any restrictions. Many of the American Federation of Labor's unions either would not admit Negroes or segregated them. The railroad brotherhoods also barred Negroes.

Negro leaders took steps to improve this labor situation. In 1920, the Friends of Negro Freedom was organized as a movement to form unions among Negro migrants from the South and fight racial discrimination in employment. Only a few local unions were formed during the three years of the Friends' existence. Next came a National Association for the Promotion of Labor Unionism among Negroes, led by A. Philip Randolph and Chandler Owen. Little progress was made and the association broke up. In October, 1925, an American Negro Labor Congress held its first meeting in Chicago. The Congress sought to bring together all groups of Negro workers and farmers. It hoped to join Negroes and whites in the labor movement. In 1925, Randolph organized the first important Negro union—the Brotherhood of Sleeping Car Porters and Maids.

New Negro social movements also began during this period. Marcus Garvey formed the first mass Negro movement, the Universal Negro Improvement Association in his native Jamaica in 1914. He organized a New York branch in 1916 and by the end of World War I, according to Garvey, there were thirty branches in the United States. Garvey appealed to the Negroes' racial pride. He said that black did not stand for inferiority, but strength and beauty. He urged American Negroes to flee to Africa and unsuccessfully appealed to the League of Nations for permission to settle a colony in Africa.

Another Negro mass movement was started in 1919 by George Baker, called "Father Divine." He proposed to turn life on earth into a virtual heaven. Many poor and frustrated men and women left their churches and called Father Divine "God." He fed thousands of people, black and white, in centers known as "heavens."

ALL INDIANS born in
the territorial limits of the
United States were granted
United States citizenship
in 1924. Before then, about two-thirds of
the Indians had become citizens through
tribal treaty agreements, laws such as the
Dawes Severalty Act of 1887, naturalization,
and the granting of citizenship for World
War I "service in the Armed Forces with an
honorable discharge." The government
however, moved slowly to improve conditions for the Indians. Ten years after the
citizenship act, the Wheeler-Howard Re-
organization Act of 1934 was adopted. It
encouraged Indians to return again to tribal
ways and urged the tribes to adopt constitutions for self-rule.

The Indians, as a rule, were having hard
times. Many of those who had obtained
farms under the Severalty Act sold their
lands cheaply to whites when the twenty-
five year time limit of government control

ended. The 1934 Wheeler-Howard Act
sought to reestablish traditional tribal organizations. Tribes were permitted to set
up their own tribal governments by a majority vote of tribe members. One-third of a
tribe's adult members could obtain corpo-
rate (legally organized) charters by petition-
ing, or requesting, the Secretary of the In-
terior. A $10,000,000 fund was established
from which $250,000 loans could be made
each year to the chartered Indian groups.

Lands which were still open for public
sale were restored to tribal ownership. The
Severalty Act which awarded farm lands to
individual Indians was stopped. Those
Indians who wished to remain as farmers
were offered agricultural training. Funds of
$250,000,000 annually were scheduled for
Indian education, including vocational and
trade schools, secondary schools and col-
leges. Programs were begun for the conser-
vation and development of the lands restored to the tribes.

A Million Negroes Joined in America's War Effort

World War II saw Negroes united in America's massive attack against the Axis powers. About one million Negro men and women saw service in almost all branches of the nation's armed forces. Though Negroes were employed in many types of jobs, segregation and discriminating practices were found in many American military areas.

William E. B. DuBois told Negroes: "If Hitler wins, every single right we now possess, for which we have struggled here in America for more than three centuries, will be instantaneously (immediately) wiped out. If the Allies win, we shall at least have the right to continue fighting for our share of democracy."

From the start, Negroes fought alongside fellow Americans to make sure the Axis did not win. On December 7, 1941, when Japanese planes attacked Pearl Harbor, Dorie Miller of Waco, Texas, a messman on the *USS Arizona*, manned a machine gun and shot down four Japanese planes. He was awarded the Navy Cross. Many other Negroes won medals for bravery in World War II battles on all fronts.

Large numbers of Negroes won commissions as officers after the War Department ordered that Negroes and whites should be admitted to the same officer candidate schools under the same qualification rules. An average of 200 new Negro officers graduated each month. The Navy, Marine Corps and Coast Guard—previously highly restricted—also commissioned some Negroes as officers. Four Negro captains commanded ships in the United States Merchant Marine.

Negro troops had to serve in segregated units. Negroes formed their own combat units, service groups and air squadrons. Strong protests brought changes in the navy's racial policy and more Negroes were enlisted and given general ratings. By 1946 the Navy had integrated its ships and bases. For the first time, Marine Corps ranks were opened to Negroes.

Franklin Roosevelt ordered equal job chances

AS AMERICA'S industry expanded to produce the materials for World War II, Negro and other non-white workers saw new opportunities. But their opportunities were limited. Before the outbreak of the war, Negroes, as did many whites, had much trouble in obtaining jobs. About 5,000,000 white workers were unemployed, and were the first to be hired. Negro leaders rose in protest. A. Philip Randolph, president of the Brotherhood of Sleeping Car Porters, in 1941 proposed to assemble 10,000 Negroes to march on Washington and demand that the government take steps to give Negroes jobs in the war industries.

Despite the urging of white leaders, Randolph refused to call off the march. Finally, President Franklin D. Roosevelt held a conference with Randolph and the Secretaries of War and Navy. Roosevelt offered to issue a positive order that could not be disobeyed, if Randolph would call off the march. On June 25, 1941, the President issued this executive order: "There shall be no discrimination in the employment of workers in defense industries or government because of race, creed, color, or national origin...And it is the duty of employers and of labor organizations...to provide for the full and equitable (equal) participation (taking part) of all workers in defense industries, without discrimination."

Roosevelt also ordered anti-discrimination clauses to be included in all defense contracts and a Committee on Fair Employment Practices to be created. Although meeting with strong opposition, mostly in the South, all the President's orders were put into effect. The Negroes' role in World War II production was strengthened. Training programs to improve Negro workers' skills were conducted by the U.S. Office of Education, a Vocational Training for War Production Workers, and an Engineering, Science and Management War Training Program. The Fair Employment Practices Committee, while meeting opposition, was successful in increasing the numbers of Negroes in war industry and government service. The aircraft industry increased Negro employment from almost none to many thousands. The iron and steel industries and the shipyards also showed great gains in Negro employment. Negroes gained increased standing in some labor unions, such as the United Steelworkers, United Mine Workers, and the National Maritime Union.

DuBois saw many racial problems after World War II

IN A SPEECH delivered after World War II, William E. B. DuBois presented his views on America's racial problems. He said: "It is with great regret that I do not see after this war, or within any reasonable time, the possibility (chance) of a world without race conflict (fighting); and this is true despite the fact that race conflict is playing a fatal (deadly) role in the modern world. The super-tragedy (greatest sorrow) of this war is the treatment of the Jews in Germany. There has been nothing comparable (equal) to this in modern history. Yet its technique (methods) and its reasoning have been based upon a race philosophy (belief) similar to that which has dominated (ruled) both Great Britain and the United States in relation to colored people...

"**In the United States** the race problem is peculiarly important just now. We see today a combination of northern investors and southern Bourbons (politicans) desiring not simply to overthrow the New Deal but to plunge the United States into fatal reaction (turning back). The power of the southerners arises from the suppression (holding back) of the Negro and poor-white vote... Nothing can be done about this situation until we face fairly the question of color discrimination in the South; until the social, political and economic equality of civilized men is recognized, despite race, color, and poverty...

"**We must then,** first, have wide dissemination (spreading) of truth. But this is not all: we need deliberate (thoughtful) and organized action on the front where race friction is being used to prolong (continue) economic inequality (unfair distribution of money) and injustice in the world... We need a concerted (united) and determined (strong) effort to make common knowledge of the facts of the distribution (division) of property and income today among individ-

uals... Next, we need organized effort to release the colored laborer from the domination (control) of the investor (person with money). This can best be accomplished by the organization of the labor of the world as consumers (users of goods), replacing the producer attitude (policy) by knowledge of consumer needs (public's needs).

"**There is a third path;** the extrication (freeing) of the poverty-stricken, ignorant laborer and consumer from his bondage by his own efforts as a worker and consumer, united to increase the price of his toil (work) and reduce the cost of the necessities of life... A union of economic liberals across the race line, with the object of driving exploiting investors (using others for own purposes) from their hideout behind race discrimination, by freeing thought and action in colonial areas is the only realistic (true) path to permanent (lasting) peace today."

Truman's civil rights program failed in Congress

HARRY S. TRUMAN was the first President to propose full entry by the federal government into the field of civil rights. In 1946, he appointed a committee to propose "more adequate and effective means and procedures (steps) for the protection of the civil rights of the people of the United States." On February 2, 1948, Truman made the recommendations, or proposals, in a civil rights message to Congress. The President's program included the following:

1. Establishing a permanent Commission on Civil Rights, a Joint Congressional Committee on Civil Rights, and a Civil Rights Division in the Department of Justice.
2. Strengthening existing civil rights laws.
3. Providing federal protection against lynching.
4. Protecting more adequately (completely) the right to vote.
5. Establishing a Fair Employment Practice Commission to prevent unfair discrimination (differences) in employment (jobs).
6. Prohibiting discrimination in interstate transportation (travel) facilities (trains, buses, planes, etc.).
7. Providing home rule and suffrage (voting rights) in Presidential elections for the residents of the District of Columbia.

8. Providing statehood for Hawaii and Alaska and a greater measure (amount) of self-government for our island possessions.
9. Equalizing the opportunities for residents of the United States to become naturalized citizens.
10. Settling the evacuation (removal) claims of Japanese Americans (after World War II).

Truman's civil rights program, coming in a Presidential election year, caused some Southern Democrats to leave the party. They were called Dixiecrats. Truman was reelected President, but was unable to push his Civil Rights program through Congress. Southern Democrats and some Republican leaders united to stop him. Efforts to force a Fair Employment Practice Commission bill through the Senate in 1950 failed when action was prevented by a filibuster, or long and unlimited speechmaking.

Truman
ordered end
of segregation
in armed forces

PRESIDENT TRUMAN issued an executive order in 1948, whose purpose was to end segregation in the armed forces of the United States. It was Executive Order 9981, and said: "It is hereby declared to be the policy of the President that there shall be equality of treatment and opportunity for all persons in the armed services without regard to race, color, religion or national origin. This policy shall be put into effect as rapidly as possible, having regard to the time required to effectuate (make) any necessary changes without impairing (reducing) efficiency or morale (spirit)." The Navy and Coast Guard had already ended segregation by 1946.

The war in Korea broke out in 1950, and America's military integration faced a test under battle conditions. A moment of great decision faced the commanding officer of the Ninth United States Infantry Regiment. The Communist North Korean enemy was strongly attacking his regiment. The commanding officer called on troops of his all-Negro Third Battalion. The Negro soldiers moved in among the whites and they fought shoulder to shoulder. The white soldiers greeted their black comrades-at-arms with relief. Together, they forced the enemy back.

After relieving General Douglas MacArthur as commander of Far Eastern forces, General Matthew Ridgway asked the Defense Department for permission to integrate all troops under his command. In four months—between May and August, 1951—the integration of U.S. forces in Korea increased from 9 per cent to 30 per cent. The army issued a report stating that the integration of Negroes had given the army greater strength and efficiency. Segregated units in the armed forces finally were ended.

Fight against discrimination spread into many fields
THE ATTACK on discrimination against Negroes spread into other fields. In 1948, the Supreme Court ruled that restrictive covenants (agreements on segregation) in public housing could not be enforced. By 1950, 177 local housing projects were open to families of all races. Nine states passed laws against discrimination in public housing. But despite the Supreme Court decision and other steps which ultimately were to lead to a federal open housing law, Negro families still had trouble in obtaining housing rights. In some neighborhoods where Negro families attempted to move in, there was violence.

The segregation of Negroes on sleeping and dining cars in interstate travel was hit by another Supreme Court decision in 1950. In the case of *Henderson* versus *United States,* the Supreme Court ruled that such segregation violated the Interstate Commerce Act, declaring it "unlawful for any railway engaged in interstate (between states) commerce to subject any particular person...to any undue or unreasonable prejudice (unfairness) or disadvantage in any respect whatever."

White primaries in the South also came under attack by the courts. The white Primary was a preliminary election to pick candidates for the general election. They were called "white primaries" because the voting laws of the particular state did not permit, or limited, Negroes' rights to vote. In 1947, a federal district court ruled that Negroes could not be kept from voting in a Democratic primary in South Carolina. About 35,000 Negroes voted in the South Carolina Democratic primary the next year. In the North, Negroes steadily added to their political power as voting drives increased the number eligible to vote. In some major cities the Negro vote sometimes decided close elections.

IMPORTANT STEPS to break down the school segregation of Negro and white children were taken by the Supreme Court headed by Chief Justice Fred Vinson. Fifty-three years had passed since 1896 when the Supreme Court had established a "separate but equal" doctrine in its *Plessy* versus *Ferguson* decision. In 1949 the Supreme Court heard a case —*Sweatt* versus *Painter*—in which a Negro sought to enter the law school at the all-white University of Texas. The court in making its decision, compared the education provided in a segregated Negro college, with the law education available at the University of Texas. The court decided that the educations were separate but *not* equal. The Negro's admission to the state law school was ordered.

In 1950, the U.S. Supreme Court took another step against school segregation. This case was *McLaurin* versus *Oklahoma State Regents*. A Negro graduate student, upon admittance to the University of Oklahoma, was required to sit at separate tables in classrooms and dining rooms. The court ruled against the university on the grounds that the Negro was deprived of a fair chance to study and to discuss matters with other students.

A 1938 decision by the Supreme Court, headed by Chief Justice Charles E. Hughes, had already ordered the state of Missouri to admit a Negro to the state university law school. The court ruled that the Negro could not be kept out since he would then be forced to attend an out-of-state law school, paying full admission and tuition charges. The Supreme Court now began to look more deeply into the "separate but equal" doctrine of segregated facilities.

new court decision opened the way for a program of school integration.

Before reaching its decision, the court took into consideration cases from four states—Kansas, South Carolina, Virginia and Delaware. The ruling, written by Chief Justice Earl Warren, said: "The plaintiffs (those who brought the suits) contend that segregated public schools are not 'equal' and cannot be made 'equal' and hence (therefore) they are deprived of (denied) the equal protection of the laws... We must consider public education in the light of its full development and its present place in American life throughout the nation... It (education) is the very foundation of good citizenship. Today it is a principal instrument (tool) in awakening him for later professional training, and helping him to adjust normally (get used to) to his environment (where he lives or works)...

"We conclude that in the field of public education the doctrine of 'separate but equal' has no place. Separate educational facilities (schools) are inherently (by nature) unequal. Therefore, we hold (decide) that the plaintiffs (the people who brought the suits) and others similarly situated for whom the actions have been brought are, by reason of the segregation complained of, deprived of the equal protection of the laws guaranteed by the Fourteenth Amendment..."

The Supreme Court on May 31, 1955, made a follow-up ruling that desegregation of the schools must be carried out with "all deliberate (thoughtful) speed." Federal District Courts were ordered to uphold the integration decree and to stamp out racial discrimination in the schools. The desegregation ruling applied to all public schools. On November 7, 1955, the Interstate Commerce Commission followed the Supreme Court's school policy by ruling that segregation on interstate buses and trains ("Jim Crow" laws) also was illegal.

Supreme Court ordered school segregation ended ALL SEGREGATION of white and Negro children in public schools was declared unconstitutional, or not in agreement with the Constitution, in a decision handed down by the U.S. Supreme Court in May, 1954. The decision did away completely with the "separate but equal" decision set forth by the Supreme Court ruling in *Plessy* versus *Ferguson* in 1896. The 1954 case which brought the court's change of opinion was *Brown* versus *Board of Education of Topeka* (Kansas). The new ruling said that laws requiring Negroes to attend separate schools violated, or were against, the Fourteenth Amendment by denying equal educational rights. The

Segregated seating caused bus boycott in Alabama

NEGROES BEGAN large scale demonstrations to end segregation in the South. In Montgomery, Alabama, Negroes boycotted, or refused to ride on, buses because of segregated seats. The boycott began on December 5, 1955, following a Negro woman's refusal to give up her seat to a white person. The woman, Mrs. Rosa Parks, a dressmaker, was arrested and fined $10. Negro riders began their boycott, led by the Reverend Martin Luther King, Jr. The bus company lost much money as the boycott continued for a year. Disorders caused Montgomery city officials at one point to declare a temporary 5 P.M. curfew, or halt, on bus service. The boycott ended in December, 1956, when a federal court issued an injunction, or order, against the further use of segregated seating.

Negroes also boycotted buses in Tallahassee, Florida, for seven months. This boycott ended after the injunction was issued in Montgomery, Alabama. Similar troubles broke out in Birmingham, Alabama. Twenty-one Negroes were arrested there for taking bus seats in a section set apart for white riders. The National Association for the Advancement of Colored People (N.A.A.C.P.) was a leader in the desegregation campaign. Martin Luther King led in organizing the boycotts.

Act of 1957 was to enforce the right to vote, regardless of race, color, national origin or religion. The Attorney General was given the power to seek court orders when individuals were denied their right to vote.

The new Civil Rights Commission was composed of six members, including no more than three members from the same political party. The commission was given the power to investigate charges that any citizen was denied his voting rights. However, the commission was to hear in closed, or secret, meeting any testimony that might unfairly criticize anyone. Witnesses to the commission hearing were limited to the state where the hearing was being held. The commission was directed to make progress reports to the President and Congress. In November, 1957, Eisenhower appointed retired Supreme Court Justice Stanley F. Reed as chairman of the commission. President John A. Hannah of Michigan State University was named vice-chairman.

Contempt of court proceedings were the only means of enforcing the 1957 act. Contempt, or lack of respect for the hearing commission, proceedings could be brought when the law was violated, or broken. The strongest punishment was $1,000 fine, or six months in jail. Jury trials were not required when the fine involved was no more than $300 and the jail sentence did not exceed 45 days.

Another section of the 1957 Civil Rights Act ended the 1866 law that gave the power to use federal troops to enforce civil rights laws. In 1960, another civil rights act was passed, authorizing judges to appoint referees to help Negroes register and vote. The Senate in 1960 approved a proposed amendment ending the payment of a special poll tax as a requirement for voting. But the judiciary committee in the House of Representatives stopped the poll tax bill from being voted on—thereby killing it for the time being.

Civil Rights Act of 1957 created a commission THE FIRST FEDERAL civil rights act since 1875 was passed on September 9, 1957, during the administration of President Dwight D. Eisenhower. The 1957 act created a bi-partisan, or two-party, executive Commission on Civil Rights. A Civil Rights Division was established in the Department of Justice, headed by an Assistant Attorney General. A major provision, or section, of the Civil Rights

All-white Little Rock school was integrated

SCHOOL integration laws faced a major test at Little Rock, Arkansas, in September, 1957. With the beginning of the fall school term, the Little Rock school board announced a program of integration by slow steps. The first Negroes were to be admitted to the formerly all-white Central High School. A state court issued an injunction stopping the school board from starting integration, but a federal district judge on August 30 issued an order setting aside the injunction issued by the state court. This meant that integration had to be carried out.

On the day before school was to open on September 2, Arkansas Governor Orval M. Faubus called out the national guard "to prevent disorder." Until then, no cases of racial violence had been reported to the police. On September 4, nine Negro students were prevented from entering the school when national guardsmen and police lined up around the building. Five days later, whites turned back six Negro students attempting to enter an all-white high school in North Little Rock. At Governor Faubus' request, President Eisenhower met with the Arkansas governor at Newport, Rhode Island, on September 14. After the

meeting, Faubus said that the Supreme Court "is the law of the land and must be obeyed."

The governor did not withdraw the national guard, however, until a federal injunction forced him to do so. On September 23, school officials allowed nine Negro students to be admitted to Central High. With the national guard withdrawn, rioting broke out. The Negroes were sent home from school. President Eisenhower ordered 1,000 United States paratroopers to Little Rock to enforce the federal court order. The state guard was placed under U.S. Army control. On September 25, the Negroes were escorted, or accompanied, to and from school by U.S. troops armed with rifles and bayonets. In spite of the violence, the U.S. Supreme Court refused to allow a delay in integrating the schools. The Little Rock schools closed and remained closed throughout the 1958-1959 school year. They finally reopened in 1960 on a desegregated plan.

BLOODY anti-integration riots broke out as James H. Meredith was enrolled, as the first Negro student at the University of Mississippi. When the violence became worse on September 30-October 1, 1962, President John F. Kennedy ordered federal troops to the college town of Oxford, Mississippi. United States marshals attempted to enforce a federal court order that Meredith be enrolled. President Kennedy made a TV address appealing to the Mississippi students to avoid violence. While the President was talking, the students fought with the marshals and two men were killed. Before the rioting ended, seventy-five were injured and 112 of the rioters were arrested. But the opposition to Meredith was not over.

Governor Ross Barnett of Mississippi led the fight to keep Meredith from entering the University of Mississippi. He had disobeyed a Federal court order to admit Meredith, a twenty-nine year old Air Force veteran. The government order was issued by a board of eight federal judges at New Orleans. Meredith was denied admittance three times, once by Governor Barnett personally. On September 26, Meredith, accompanied by five cars filled with United States marshals, was forced back by 400 Mississippi highway patrolmen. Additional marshals and airborne federal troops were rushed to Oxford. On September 30, the President ordered that enough troops be sent to enforce the court's order. At the height of the disorders, an estimated 15,000 federal troops were in Oxford, Mississippi.

On the night of September 30, widespread rioting took place throughout the town of Oxford. The troops used bayonets and tear gas, but fired their rifles over the rioters' heads as they put down the disorders. Governor Barnett, meanwhile, gave in to the court order and urged that peace be restored. On October 1, Meredith was enrolled and was led by marshals as he entered buildings to attend his first classes. Governor Barnett was accused of contempt of court by the federal court. Former Army Major General Edwin Walker, who had commanded the troops sent to Little Rock to enforce school desegregation, took an opposite role in the events at Oxford. He urged Mississippians to stand up against the U.S. troops at Oxford—even offering to lead the resistance. Walker appeared at the scene of the riots and was arrested on charges of "inciting (urging) to rebellion."

"sit-in" at North Carolina store started a movement THE NEGROES' modern revolution for civil rights went into full action at the Negro Agricultural and Technical College at Greensboro, North Carolina, on February 1, 1960. On that day, four Negro students entered a store, made some purchases, and ordered coffee. Upon being refused service because they were Negroes, the four students "sat in" at the lunch counter until the store closed. The "sit-in" movement spread and the revolution for civil rights swept across the South. By this time some civil rights gains had been made—in integration, voting and interstate transportation. But other rights had not yet been won.

Disorders broke out at Birmingham, Alabama, in 1961, when white and Negro Freedom Riders were attacked as they rode in buses to test the U.S. law that made separate seating illegal while traveling from one state to another. Other civil rights demonstrations took place at Birmingham. Thousands of Negroes, including many school children, staged a march in May, 1963. Police used fire hoses and police dogs to stop the march and arrested many for "parading without a permit."

Four Negro girls attending a Birmingham Sunday school were killed by a bomb on September 15, 1963. It was the 21st time in eight years that Negroes had been the targets of bombing. This latest episode caused angry Negro riots in Birmingham's streets.

In June, 1963, Governor George Wallace stood in a building doorway to stop two Negro students from entering the University of Alabama at Tuscaloosa. Wallace refused to permit them to enter. President Kennedy immediately signed an order federalizing the Alabama national guard (attaching them to the U.S. Army). In a second meeting at the doorway later in the day, Wallace withdrew and the two Negroes

were registered at the University.

By 1963, Mississippi remained as the only Southern state without any Negro students integrated into its white elementary and secondary schools. Both white and black men and women had suffered violence and shootings to promote civil rights in Mississippi. On June 12, 1963, Medgar Evers, the N.A.A.C.P.'s Mississippi state chairman, was killed by a sniper as he entered his home at Jackson. Evers' accused slayer was freed when court proceedings in 1964 twice ended in mistrials.

ity in job opportunities and the ending of discrimination in working conditions were high on the list of Freedom March goals.

The thousands of marchers traveled from as far away as the West Coast. In many cases, planes and special trains were rented to bring the marchers to Washington. The highways leading into Washington were jammed with autos and buses. The huge gathering and demonstration were completely peaceful.

In the capital, the marchers gathered at the Washington Monument, while thirteen of their leaders called on members of Congress. At that time, Congress was considering a new civil rights law. The marchers moved down Constitution Avenue to the Lincoln Memorial. There, earnest speeches outlining Negroes' goals were made. President John F. Kennedy later said: "The cause of 20 million Negroes has been advanced by the program before the Lincoln Memorial."

Kennedy used his office to bring in and advance many Negroes in the federal government. He appointed Negroes to several important federal judiciary positions. He named as judges Thurgood Marshall to the New York circuit court, and Wade McCree to the district court for Eastern Michigan. Lyndon B. Johnson, on becoming President after the assassination of Kennedy, also supported increased Negro participation in the federal government. He appointed Circuit Judge Thurgood Marshall as Solicitor General of the United States. He promoted Wade McCree from the U.S. district court to the circuit court. President Johnson also appointed Robert Weaver as secretary of the new Department of Housing and Urban Development, the first Negro to become a member of the President's cabinet. Other Negro appointments were George L. P. Weaver as Assistant Secretary of Labor and Carl Rowan as Deputy Assistant Secretary of State.

200,000 took part in Washington Freedom March

A FREEDOM MARCH on Washington carried to the nation's capital a direct plea for the recognition by both government and the people of the civil rights crusade. On August 28, 1963, approximately 200,000 persons took part in the march. The great majority were Negroes, but thousands of whites joined in. Some 200 religious leaders—Protestant, Catholic, Jewish—joined in the demonstration. Two of the Negroes' outstanding leaders held major roles in planning the march—Martin Luther King, Jr., and A. Philip Randolph, the recognized leader of the Negro labor movement. Equal-

1964 Act Was Strong Gain in Civil Rights Movement

The Civil Rights Act of 1964 was a major step in the fight for equality. The act was based on legislation submitted to Congress in 1963 by John F. Kennedy. Lyndon Johnson, upon becoming President after Kennedy's assassination, urged Congress to pass the bill to honor Kennedy's memory. Congress passed the bill and President Johnson signed it into law on July 2, 1964.

The 1964 act ruled out discrimination in public services on grounds of race, color, religion or national origin. Negroes were guaranteed equal services in such public places as hotels, restaurants, lunch counters, theaters and halls for concerts.

Equal opportunity in obtaining and holding jobs, regardless of race, color or sex, was ordered. Discrimination in labor unions was forbidden. An Equal Employment Opportunity Commission took over.

The Attorney General was authorized to file court suits to enforce school desegregation. The law did not authorize courts or U.S. officials to order transportation of children from one school to another merely for the purposes of integration.

Any program or activity which received federal financial, or money, assistance faced the loss of such money if the laws against racial discrimination were broken by the organization receiving funds.

Voting Act of 1965 Swept Away Blocks to the Polls

The Voting Rights Act of 1965 was aimed to stop methods which denied Negroes an opportunity to vote. In signing the bill into law on August 6, President Johnson said the act "strikes away the last major shackle (slavery chain)."

The "examiners" could talk with those wishing to vote and, if they were found qualified as voters, order their registration on the voting lists so they would be allowed to vote on election day.

The act authorized the appointment of federal "examiners," or registrars, to assure the enrollment of all qualified voters in federal, state and local elections—regardless of race, creed or color.

Literacy tests which were unfair and had been used to deny Negroes their voting rights were ordered stopped. The day after the act became law, the U.S. Justice Department stopped such tests in seven Southern states and Alaska.

The Twenty-fourth Amendment, ratified in 1964, ended the poll(voting) tax, or any other tax, as a requirement for voting in national elections. The 1965 act declared that such taxes were wrong since they denied an individual his constitutional right to vote in any election, including state elections. Suits were filed against poll tax laws in effect in Mississippi, Alabama, Texas and Virginia.

Nearly 1,000,000 more Negro voters were registered in eleven Southern states from 1964 to May, 1968. In 1964 there were 2,164,000 Negroes registered. The total increased to 2,189,000 in 1967 and rose to 3,072,000 in 1968. This showed increased Negro voting power at the polls.

Civil Disorders Commission Called for Reforms

In March, 1968, a report was made by an Advisory Commission on Civil Disorders which President Johnson named in 1967. The commission, headed by Governor Otto Kerner of Illinois, said: "Our nation is moving toward two societies, one black, one white—separate and unequal." A program of reforms costing billions of dollars was proposed by the Kerner report. White racism and poor Negro living conditions were blamed for much violence.

Proposals in the report also included the building of 6 million units of good, clean housing for lower-income groups. Also proposed was an "open occupancy" law, outlawing discrimination in housing.

Total desegregation and more pre-school and vocational, or job-training, courses were educational goals for the program.

The commission said that 2 million equal opportunity jobs should be created. It set welfare standards at a "minimum (lowest) poverty" level of $3,335 a year. It was proposed that Negroes have a larger share in deciding neighborhood policy.

An open occupancy law was passed soon after the report was issued. It made illegal all racial discrimination in the sale and rental of 80 per cent of the houses and apartments in the United States.

Wave of riots, violence brought on investigation

THE SPECIAL Advisory Commission on Civil Disorders issued its report as the result of an investigation of riots during 1967.

Martin Luther King had warned that the summer of 1967 could bring bloody disorders. His warning had come true in massive riots at Newark, New Jersey, on July 12-17 and at Detroit on July 23-30. In both cities firebombing, property damage, shootings, and arrests took place. In the Newark riot, 26 were killed, 1,500 injured, and 1,000 arrested. At Detroit, 43 Negroes and whites were killed and 2,000 were injured. It was after the Newark and Detroit riots that President Johnson named the commission.

Violence and riots had been on the rise since 1964. In the summer of 1964, three young men, two whites and one Negro, had been killed while working on a voter registration program in Mississippi. Their bodies were found in a shallow grave near the small town of Philadelphia, Mississippi. A federal jury convicted seven suspects, including a Klan leader, of the killings.

Martin Luther King in 1965 had led civil rights groups in a three-months voter registration demonstration at Selma, Alabama. There had been several killings during the campaign. Thirty-five persons, including policemen, were killed in riots in the Negro Watts area of Los Angeles in August 1965. James Meredith, who was the first Negro to enroll in the University of Mississippi, was shot on June 6, 1966, while making a personal voting drive march in Mississippi. He received several wounds, but recovered and continued his march.

Rioting had also taken place in the North in the summer of 1966. Disorders occurred in Negro sections of Chicago, Cleveland and New York City. Two were killed in Cleveland and two others died in Chicago during an open housing march.

In complete contrast to the rioting was a peaceful campaign at Resurrection City. Also called Poor City, Resurrection City was a camp built alongside the reflection pool near the Lincoln Memorial in Washington. From May 5 to June 25, 1968, thousands of poor peoples' campaigners, led by the Reverend Ralph D. Abernathy, worked out of Resurrection City. They sought new relief measures for America's poor.

"Black Power" Became a New Civil Rights Force

The phrase "Black Power" was first used in 1966. Soon many blacks called for the removal of all whites from their organizations. Black Power became a powerful force in civil rights. Many black groups defined Black Power in their own way.

The Congress of Racial Equality was formed to push voter registration drives in the South. "Black Power," said CORE President Floyd McKissick, "seeks power in the areas of politics, economics, self-image, leadership, law enforcement and consumer buying. United, the black man can fight the evil of white supremacy." Schools were set up to teach black culture, heritage and art to ghetto children.

Stokely Carmichael, the chairman of SNCC, a civil rights organization, led many Black Power drives. "Black Power," said Carmichael, "is to provide a community with a position of strength from which to make its voice heard...to win political power and move on into activities that would have economic effects. This is what blacks seek: control. Ultimately the economic foundation of this country must be shaken if black people are to control their lives. For racism to die, a totally new America must be born!"

One of the oldest Black Power groups, the Black Muslims, called for complete separation of white and black communities. The Muslims used only their own restaurants, grocery stores and police to avoid any need of the white man. Muslim followers took new names and gave up all alcohol, tobacco and cosmetics. Women wore special dress and children went to special Muslim schools.

Charles Hamilton, college professor and writer for the Black Power movement, said Black Power is "talking about a drastic change in the nature of the social-political system—its values as well as institutions. For the black people of the ghetto, the system is no longer legitimate. The fact is that black people have the power to deny peace and stability to the larger society. Only when black people feel a personal stake in the society will they protect it. Only then will it be legitimate."

Rise of Negro Leaders Gained Voters' Support

At an increasing rate, American voters supported political candidates regardless of color or race. Negro candidates in many cities were fully accepted and won elections with substantial support of white voters.

Edward W. Brooke was elected in 1966 by Massachusetts voters as the first Negro member of the U. S. Senate in the Twentieth Century. Brooke, one of the most popular Republicans in the state, defeated former Governor Endicott Peabody in the 1966 Massachusetts election.

Thurgood Marshall was sworn in on October 2, 1967, as the first Negro member of the U.S. Supreme Court. Marshall was appointed by President Johnson while serving as Solicitor General of the United States. Marshall had once been special attorney for the National Association for the Advancement of Colored People.

Negro candidates won voter support and were elected in congressional and local elections. Mrs. Shirley Chisholm of Brooklyn, New York, was elected in 1968 as the first Negro woman to become a member of Congress. In 1967, Cleveland voters elected Carl B. Stokes as mayor, and Gary, Indiana, elected Richard G. Hatcher as mayor. In 1969, Charles Evers was elected as the mayor in Fayetteville, Mississippi.

Tragedy struck on April 4, 1968, when Martin Luther King was assassinated at Memphis, Tenn. King, prominent civil rights leader, was shot by James Earl Ray on the balcony of a motel while discussing plans for a civil rights march. The Reverend Ralph Abernathy was with King at the time of King's shooting. Abernathy became the new leader of the Southern Christian Leadership Conference.

The Fight for Rights Covered Many Fronts

College students used the rights of free speech in a wave of protest demonstrations and disorders on many campuses in 1968-1969. The students demanded more academic freedoms, or voice in college affairs. They claimed the right to have a voice in the choice of faculty members and courses to be studied, including special courses in Negro history.

The right to free speech did not apply when violent means were used to express beliefs, the Supreme Court ruled in a Bluefield (West Virginia) State College case. The court upheld the suspensions of ten students who had staged a violent demonstration. In another case the Supreme Court freed forty persons who had been convicted of disorderly conduct. The court ruled the protesters had a right to stage a non-violent demonstration.

A high degree of integration of America's armed forces saw Negroes fighting shoulder-to-shoulder with whites in Viet Nam. Integration of all military units gave many opportunities for Negro advancement. Some units of white and Negro soldiers were commanded by Negro officers. Frederic Davison, a Negro colonel, was promoted to brigadier genneral while leading white and black troops in combat operations in Viet Nam.

Robert L. Bennett, U.S. Commissioner of Indian Affairs, said: "The overriding (main) Indian problem is continuing poverty." The U.S. began a public works program on reservations to give Indians more job opportunities. Puerto Ricans and Mexican-Americans fought for greater job and educational chances and better housing, to provide a better living.

Glossary

Abridged (*a bridged'*). Cut down, reduced.

Academic freedom (*ack' e dem ic, free' dom*). Right to express opinions freely in college affairs.

Amendment (*a mend' ment*). Change in or addition to the Constitution.

Contempt of Court. Lack of respect or disobeying order—open to punishment by the court.

Crusade (*cru sade'*). A fight, or campaign, to gain a goal.

Demonstration (*dem' on stra shun*). Public action to attract attention.

Discrimination (*dis crim' i na shun*). Denying rights of others because of unfair beliefs.

Dissenting (*dis sent' ing*). Disagreeing with.

Doctrine (*doc' trine*). A belief, or policy.

Domination (*dom' i na' shun*). Strong rule over somebody or something.

Due process of law. Taking proper steps, in order, as called for by the laws.

Inciting (*in cit' ing*). Urging or causing somebody to do something.

Injunction (*in junc' shun*). A court order against some action.

Integrity (*in teg' ri ty*). Honesty of purpose, true value.

Integration (*in' te gra' shun*). Giving whites and non-whites the same service in the same place.

Jurisdiction (*ju ris dic' shun*). Control over, government.

Literacy (*lit' er a cy*). Ability to read and write.

Manifesto (*mani' i fes' to*). Declaration of policy or plans.

Migration (*mi gra' shun*). Persons moving toward some place.

Nullify (*nul' i fy*). Kill, erase.

Occupancy (*oc' cu pan cy*). Living or working in some place.

Persecution (*per' se cu' shun*). Unfair or cruel treatment.

Prejudices (*prej' u dices*). Unfair beliefs or actions.

Racial (*ra' cial*). Involving two or more races or people.

Ratified (*rat' i fied*). Approved by three-fourths of the states.

Segregation (*seg' re ga' shun*). Keeping whites and non-whites in separate places for services, such as schools.

Suffrage (*suf' frage*). The right to vote.

Unalienable (*un al' ien a ble*). Cannot be taken away.

Underground railroad (*un' der ground', rail' road*). The term used to mean secret systems of helping slaves escape.

Chronology

Laws enacted to guarantee rights of
the American people

CIVIL RIGHTS

1866 Civil Rights Act of 1866 guaranteed equal rights regardless of race, color, religion or national origin.

1868 Fourteenth Amendment gave Negroes U.S. citizenship and equal civil rights.

1924 Indian Citizenship Act gave all Indians born in the United States U.S. citizenship.

1954 The Supreme Court ruled that school segregation violated the Constitution. Integration was ordered.

1955 The Interstate Commerce Commission prohibited segregated seating in interstate buses and trains.

1964 Civil Rights Act of 1964 ordered equal treatment of Negroes in employment, voting and public services at such places as hotels, restaurants and theaters.

1964 Civil Rights Act of 1964 (Title VII) prohibited discrimination in employment on grounds of race, color, religion, sex, or national origin. Refusal to hire a worker because of color or sex was declared illegal, as were exclusion or expulsion from union membership.

1968 Open Occupancy Law prohibited racial discrimination in the sale or rental of 80 per cent of the nation's housing.

RIGHTS TO VOTE

1870 The Fifteenth Amendment gave Negroes voting rights.

1920 The Nineteenth Amendment gave women full voting rights.

1957 Civil Rights Commission was created to protect Negroes' rights to vote.

1964 Twenty-fourth Amendment prohibited poll tax, or registration fee, as a requirement for voting in national elections. State poll tax laws were challenged in court.

1965 Voting Rights Law suspended literacy tests as a requirement for voting eligibility. Federal supervisors were authorized to register Negro voters.

INDEX